DISHING THE DIRT

First published by Canbury Press 2020
This edition published 2020

Canbury Press
Kingston upon Thames, Surrey, United Kingdom
www.canburypress.com

Printed in Great Britain by CPI Group (UK) Ltd, Croydon
Cover: Alice Marwick

This is a work of non-fiction.

Typeset by Canbury Press
9.5/14 Narbero Serif and Mr Eaves XL Mod OT 14/12

ISBN
Paperback: 978-1-912454-46-4
Ebook: 978-1-912454-47-1
PDF: 978-1-912454-49-5
Audiobook: 978-1-912454-48-8

DISHING THE DIRT

Nick Duerden

AUTHOR'S NOTE

Demand for domestic cleaners has never been higher. If we don't employ one ourselves, we probably know someone who does. Comparatively few people, however, know much about the workers themselves.

In the autumn of 2018, I set out to find out more about the individuals who play such an intimate role in our homes. Over 15 months, I interviewed dozens of cleaners from all over the world who have settled, and now work, in London, and I asked them about their lives. At first many were understandably nervous and mistrustful, and reluctant to talk; others spoke as if they had been waiting for years to be heard.

Each chapter of this book offers a glimpse into a previously hidden world, a selection of snapshots that reveal what it's really like to clean up after others in a country that's often far from home, where cultural disparities loom large, and where homeowners can have peculiarly exacting standards.

For reasons that will become obvious, some names have been changed.

Contents

Advert on Gumtree for domestic cleaning services

Hello

This is Taki and Simone at jobs done

plus the guys from the WhatsApp Cleaning group

Im Not A Agency Or work for a Company

Taki & Simone are cousins which are cleaner that got too many jobs and now have set up a WhatsApp group with other cleaner and we share and swap jobs

I have trained all the cleaners my self personally as I have very high standards not just in the service of work but in Customer service

Are you still looking for a amazing cleaner ;)

This is what Is willing to be Done as long as time permits

How many hours do you need ?

If there is a Pacific room or area you want concentrating on please let me know

– Floor will be hover and moped

– cooker Top will be cleaned

– Any dishes done and put away

BATHROOMS/SHOWERS/TOILETS Cleaning

– Windows will be clean (indoor only)

– All floors clean/carpet/mopped

– Bed made all new sets changed and made

– Any built in cupboards are cleaned externally

I'm organised and reliable I sometime do these services With other cleaners at the price which will allow me finish the job quicker because we are working as a team

Prologue. Clocking On

It was as if she were invisible, like she wasn't even there. Or, perhaps more accurately, like she didn't really count, not in any tangible sense, this mostly silent domestic cleaner with the broken English whose back was perpetually stooped over the vacuum cleaner, the dustpan and brush, the damp mop; someone who likely knew her way around the utility room better than the homeowners themselves.

Today, the wife was away on business, as she frequently was, but the husband wasn't here alone. The marital bed was not empty.

'A different woman,' she says. 'Younger.'

And he didn't hide this from you, wasn't embarrassed, ashamed of parading his affair so brazenly under your nose?

She shakes her head, and smiles tightly. 'No,' she says. 'No.'

She was seemingly in his confidence, then, but not through any prior agreement, a finger to the side of the nose, and nor was he paying her for her silence, her implicit complicity. 'I don't think he even considered me,' she says. 'Or my reaction.' She was merely part of the furniture, a once-weekly presence in the house who mutely got on with her work as she always did, over three floors, three bedrooms and two bathrooms: the vacuuming, the polishing, the dusting.

She had a name, Boglárka, and she was Hungarian, mid-thirties, here in London a couple of years now, almost fluent but shy with it. She had a bank account, a bike, an Oyster card; she flat-shared in one of the outer boroughs, and diligently sent money back home each month via PayPal. The wife knew her name, though would, like everyone else here, struggle with its hard consonants, but the husband offered no suggestion that he did. 'Hello' and 'goodbye' had been the full extent of their communications since her work here had begun a full year previously.

Right now, she picked up the clothes that had been discarded, pre-coitally the night before, on the bedroom carpet, disposed of the used prophylactic, and focused on the post-coital bed once she—the other woman—had at last got up to join the husband downstairs in the kitchen. More traces of the previous night's indiscretion were then dutifully wiped clean, the bed stripped, the sheets bundled into the washing machine, which she set to 60° before pressing START. She cleaned the en-suite, the shower stall, and scrubbed the toilet bowl, which bore evidence of repeated use and little care and attention on the days she didn't come to clean. She hung his crumpled suit jacket back in the wardrobe, and liberated the clothes dryer of its smalls, his and his absent wife's, replacing them gently, respectfully even, in their appropriate drawers, his and hers, on either side of the matrimonial bed. The photograph of the both of them on their wedding day, confetti in their hair, sat in its usual position on the chest of drawers. She dusted it now, as she always did.

Working from the top of the house to the bottom, opening windows under the eaves in the attic and disturbing the dust, which took to the air and danced in a column of sunlight, she used Cif and Harpic, Domestos and Windolene, her rubber gloves slick with chemicals, her fingers inside clammy with sweat. Often, she was down on her hands and knees, because he liked the carpet beneath the bed swept, the floorboards underneath the sofa, too. Here, she found balls of fluff, probably the cat's, and curling sweet wrappers; she found odd socks, a random shoe whose low-heeled counterpart, she presumed, was secreted elsewhere in the house but not yet stumbled across. A bra: the wife's, or the other woman's?

If the bathroom had been reliably messy, the kitchen was worse. The kitchen was always worse. Woks and frying pans meant grease splattered north east south and west, the cupboards alongside the hob, the dust-encrusted extractor fan above. Mr Muscle Kitchen Cleaner, and lots of it. Plates were piled high in the sink, mugs with days-old tidemarks. A scouring pad somewhere beneath.

Next to the microwave, the coffee that he had made for her, that he made for her every Wednesday morning at 8 o'clock, was cooling, first ignored, then ultimately forgotten, coffee that she would, after he had departed for work, pour slowly down the sink in favour of the tall glass of water she needed to slake her mounting thirst.

She steered clear of the kitchen for now, taking her time in the living room, with its bookshelves, mantelpiece trinkets, the multiple picture frames, the Venetian blinds. She loitered here longer because they were still at the kitchen table, sharing a leisurely breakfast, her legs draped proprietorially over his. He had made her something complicated with eggs (his usual breakfast was a banana and slice of toast), and both of them would be late for work. From where she was in the lounge, deliberately not eavesdropping but overhearing everything anyway, she could make out kisses, lovers' giggles. She coughed loudly, deliberately. The ruse worked. The man looked over at the wall clock, noting the time. Shoes on, jackets, briefcase and handbag. Car keys. The front door opened, then slammed shut. Gone, leaving nothing but trails of aftershave and perfume in their wake.

She would likely never see this woman again, and next Wednesday the wife would be back in place, this woman to whom Boglárka would have to smile in greeting while maintaining an awkward silence, siding with the husband when, had she been given the choice, the option, she'd much rather have sympathised with the wife. But this was a line she was unable to cross, the ghost in the house who saw no evil, nor spoke it. Her presence in this soap opera might have been front row, but it was not her place to applaud or jeer.

But then, as she had long ago learned, this was an unwritten part of her job description. A domestic cleaner sees many things on any given day during the cleaning of houses; she—and more often than not it is a woman—tells no one. Or almost no one. She tells her fellow cleaners. Cleaners have much gossip to share, and plenty of war stories. And so while she sees everything, and sometimes bears the brunt of her employers' casual cruelties, she keeps shtum. She simply gets on with the task at hand, because there is always more work to do. Dirt has a habit of reproducing. Always more dirt, always more to clean.

Boglárka has also learned that while she would prefer to have a full grasp of English, some employers would like her tongue to remain semi-skilled. When one is not fluent in the language of the host country, her flatmates have explained, a barrier remains between employer and employee—a notable distance. The hierarchy is observed. Non-linguists can feel inhibited in such situations, so perhaps this is one reason why so many are employed in London today. Homeowners like the conviction that they are above, and cleaners below. The less likely cleaners are to answer back, the more the social order is maintained. In this way, our domestic help will keep themselves to themselves, and focus solely, and silently, on the task at hand. In this way, each can ignore the other's existence more easily, if not entirely, the physical presence of either party receding into a fuzzy background.

But our cleaners do take notice. Naturally and reflexively, they are cultural anthropologists. They hold the key to our real identities, to the people we really are, behind closed doors.

***

Domestic help, now so common, such a factor of everyday life, was once a comparative rarity in the UK, the preserve of the upper classes, those who lived upstairs and employed those who dwelt downstairs. By the early 1900s, the middle classes had begun to enjoy the benefits of cleaners, too, not merely because they also craved tidy homes that they did not have to toil over, but because employing domestic staff had become an indicator of status. The average cleaning lady was a cleaning girl, still a teenager and likely uneducated, and therefore eminently affordable; the pay was low—1p an hour was not untypical—and they often worked 16-hour days. Food and board was included, but the food the servant ate was far inferior to the food they cooked and served their employers, and they often slept in basements, or up in draughty attics, occasionally in the kitchen itself. They were extended few courtesies, and expected to never step out of line. Punishment could be harsh if they did. They had no rights, no public voice.

They were second-class citizens working as slave labour, but without them residences would fall into abject disarray. Under-appreciated as they were, their presence in so many of the nation's households was essential.

After World War Two, and the introduction of the welfare state in 1948, money was scarce and demand for cleaners evaporated. Throughout the 1950s and beyond, they became, once again, largely the preserve of the wealthy.

But the 1980s saw another shift. Increasingly, both husbands and wives were now required to go out to work, to pursue careers. This left little time for domestic upkeep, and if wives—traditionally the housekeepers—were too tired to vacuum after a long day at the office, their husbands were unlikely to step into the breach. Two salaries brought financial security, and so once again we looked to others to clean up after us. The gig economy duly materialised, and previously out-of-work women began to advertise themselves as cleaners. They brought their friends with them, their mothers and daughters. There was no shortage of willing char ladies. They advertised in the windows of local newsagents, and relied upon word-of-mouth. Business grew.

A generation on, cleaners began utilising the internet. Now anyone can find one at the click of a mouse, and many of us have done just that. Type 'cleaners London' into a search engine, and over 39 million results come up.

The 21st Century has seen further change to how we manage our daily lives. Increasingly, we are willing to delegate more, specifically to pay others to do the work we'd rather not do ourselves, even if we cannot really afford it. A wave of cheap immigrant labour entered the UK between 2000 and 2020, especially from the new EU member states in eastern Europe. Better to pay a Magda from Poland, say, £30 a week to run the Hoover around the house for a few hours than to save the money for a rainy day. This of course plays into Magda's fortunes directly, and what the profession has lost in status, it has gained in popularity. Careers can be made in cleaning now, and entrepreneurial types have rushed to set up their own businesses in what has become a booming market. Magda, meanwhile, has WhatsApped her friends back home telling of the ready work available here, and her friends, none of them workshy, have come in their droves.

One in four households today with an annual income of under £20,000 still finds the money to pay for a cleaner. Nationwide, the industry is worth some £26 billion a year. Research commissioned by the insurance company esure suggests that the under 35s are most likely to have a cleaner on a weekly basis, millennials intent on getting the most out of their downtime in a way that, by comparison, their parents never did, and never could. If there used to be a certain stigma, a lingering sense of class guilt, about employing another human being to tidy up after you when you could tidy up yourself, there isn't any more. The younger generation has grown up learning that cleaning is something one simply doesn't do for oneself. Others can do that kind of thing for you.

We might still feel secretly awkward about this. In the words of the writer and poet Kate Clanchy, who wrote a book, *Antigona and Me,* in 2009 about the improbable relationship she had with her own cleaner, a refugee from Kosovo:

'It's about class, and oppression. Even if you think of yourself as this nice, liberal person, you are still representative of the leading class, especially to those you employ. The truth is, every white person in this country is sustained by three or four brown people, and that can be embarrassing to us for all sorts of reasons.'

If it is increasingly true that more and more of our cleaners are coming from overseas—and this is nowhere more true than in London, immigrants invariably fated to do the jobs shunned by natives—then there is another, more revealing, reason why. Those who come from Poland, from Bulgaria and Romania, from the Philippines and Indonesia, tend often to be university educated. Back home, they were white-collar professionals. They had status. But they were forced to leave their countries because they could no longer afford to live, or provide for their families, on the wages they earned, even in decent jobs. Inflation was crippling. In Bulgaria, for example, electricity bills rose month on month—up to 40 per cent during the years 2017/18—which sent even fairly well-paid careerists plunging towards the breadline. So they left their breaking, and broken, countries, and travelled abroad in pursuit of that most covet-able of things: a living wage. They came to the UK, and they came to London, where the capital is full of domiciles that need cleaning, and owners impatient to employ someone to oversee the whole messy business. Many such homeowners found themselves more comfortable taking on someone from Romania than from Romford.

'If you employ a British person to clean your house, they are likely to be working class,' says one former cleaner-turned-businesswoman from Bulgaria's capital, Sofia. 'Many have studied, just like you have, to get a British education, but unlike you, they still end up a cleaner, and this is for them a low status job. So they might resent you. And you, the employer, might see this resentment, and feel it. It's a class issue, I think. It makes people uncomfortable. But if you employ someone from overseas, someone like me, then you have an educated person cleaning your house, middle-class just like you. So they are the same as you, you might say. With an English cleaner, perhaps not so much. That's the difference. And it's a big difference.'

A recent survey undertaken by Bark, a hiring website, revealed that the areas of the UK that saw the highest employment of domestic cleaners included places like Oxford, Cambridge, Reading and York; London was ranked number one. The cities that employed the fewest, and so were deemed the 'dirtiest,' were Aberdeen, Manchester, Norwich and Leeds.

The 'cleanest' boroughs in London were Kensington, Westminster, Richmond, Hammersmith and Fulham, and Camden. Without their cleaners, householders would be living in filth. Or else many of us would, like our parents before us, have to spend several evenings and most of Saturday tidying up after ourselves, always the most onerous task of the working week, and the most mundane. The idea of divorce can take root in such monotony.

Those that clean for Londoners are a silent army. They bring order to our lives, they put out the bins, and relieve us of at least some of the myriad pressures of modern life. They are privy to our indiscretions, our peculiarities, our curious habits. They put up with us, which isn't always easy because some of us are complicated souls.

But who are the members of these well-drilled regiments? What are their stories? Do they know that we talk about them when we are among ourselves—at dinner parties, at coffee mornings, at the school gates—and how much do we care that they, too, talk about us? If we are the prism through which they view their host nation, what conclusions do they draw? Do we make for decent employers, fair and kind, perhaps even generous? And if we are sometimes cruel, and talk down at them, why do we do that? Do we treat them fairly—or are they being taken advantage of?

If we asked them, what would they say?

1. The Entrepreneur

Y ou would not believe,' she says, holding my gaze and raising her plucked eyebrow into a Roger Moore arch. 'Seriously, you have no idea.'

Yuliya is Bulgarian, a former cleaner turned businesswoman. She is telling me about her first few months in this country. 'A big education,' she says. She arrived in 2007, aged 29, with her husband, leaving their three-month-old daughter at home with her mother-in-law. She didn't want to leave, but felt forced to do so. 'But I was lucky.' While she had never been to Britain before, she had friends who had settled in Surbiton, a comfortable slice of suburban London, who offered her and her husband the sofa. Surbiton prides itself on politeness and self-conscious levels of decency that newcomers like Yuliya quickly felt and immediately appreciated. She could speak English, but only just, and while she felt welcome, seeking what she calls 'a proper job' was out of the question. 'I couldn't turn up to interviews speaking such bad English,' she says. 'I couldn't.'

She became a cleaner.

Back in her hometown of Plovdiv, Yuliya had been a sales executive in an insurance company. Previously, she had studied finance and banking at one of Bulgaria's best academies. As a twentysomething, she was doing well. 'But I couldn't afford to live.' She shrugs. 'The utility bills.'

By Bulgarian standards, she had been on pretty decent money. 'Let's say you work for £1,000 a month, which is a very good wage there, but your electricity bill is £250–300 a month, and then you have to pay rent, and you have to buy food. And so every month, you have nothing left. It's difficult. And then it becomes impossible.'

Like many of her compatriots, she felt she had to move abroad for work. She had resisted doing so, until she became a parent. 'I had to do it for my little girl,' she says. Leaving her daughter behind, albeit until she and her husband were settled, was the hardest thing she had ever done. 'I passed my first few months here cleaning and crying, cleaning and crying.'

When I ask if she had cleaned houses before, back home in Bulgaria, she smiles at my wilful naivete.

'No one,' she says flatly, almost sternly, 'who comes here like I did has cleaned before. We've come from proper jobs, good jobs. But if you don't speak fluently here, then it's impossible to look for similar jobs, even with a good education. So it's better to do something and earn enough, than try to look smart but remain unemployed and not be able to pay your bills. Most of the people who come here to do cleaning have never even considered cleaning before, as all of them are well educated. I know cleaners in the UK who were teachers back at home, chemists; they worked in banks. Most of them are very well educated.'

The period of readjustment was complicated. Yuliya tells me that when you do menial work for people whose education might not be as good as yours, and they then criticise your work, it's almost impossible not to feel a little resentment. 'You just feel: Well, come on, I'm not stupid, I'm not doing this because I want to, because I haven't studied, because I'm not clever enough. I'm in this position because I was born in a country that couldn't provide for me, and I don't have a choice. So please, treat me with some respect at least.'

She says:

'Cleaning is a low status job, of course it is, and everyone goes through that pain in the beginning. You feel bad about yourself because—look! You are cleaning toilets! It's like: "why have I studied for so many years only to end up doing this?" And you know that back at home, your mother is crying because of how you have ended up. But if you have seen near-poverty in your country, as I have, you quickly come to accept it. This is your reality. You just feel: "I need to cover my bills, I need to be able to make money so that I can send money home." So you very quickly come to focus on that and stop thinking about your ego, your pride. All you think about, really, is the money. You need to make money.'

Before long, Yuliya started making money. After landing a few regular cleaning jobs, she printed up flyers, and got to know her neighbourhood more by posting them through letter boxes in and around Surbiton. Soon, she extended her reach to nearby Kingston upon Thames. It might not be factually true to suggest that everybody who walks through the streets of Kingston does so pushing a pushchair, but it might as well be. Yuliya realised that there are many families in Kingston, and many stretched parents who needed help. Before long, Yuliya was inundated with requests and bookings. While her husband was working in construction ('like all men who come here from Bulgaria'), she became skilled at her new job. Demand for her services grew.

'I learned that people wanted foreign cleaners, but specifically female cleaners,' she says. 'My ex-husband would never have done what I did. Sometimes men might be employed for one-off cleaning jobs, for particularly heavy jobs, end-of-tenancy work— which, believe me, is disgusting—but very often clients don't want a man in their house. They want women. So now, in my company, I employ only women.'

'You would not believe,' she says. 'You have no idea.'

Yuliya is talking about her early cleaning experiences, the memorably bad ones when she worked for people who showed no gratitude. Recreational drug users who left their needles on the floor, and expected her—an educated woman—to pick them up; the students who left trails of domestic destruction in their wake, and demanded she make miracles inside two hours for £20.

She sips from her Pret espresso, and sighs. 'But I very quickly stopped working for such bad clients. This was not the kind of work I wanted to do.'

She shows me photographs on her phone, evidence of kitchen and bathroom surfaces strewn with detritus and grime. 'See? They make such a mess, and they are not embarrassed, or ashamed. They just act like it's normal. Sometimes I don't understand how people can live like that, because no way is it possible. You can't imagine touching the surfaces of a kitchen like this, let alone cooking on it! Or, for me, cleaning it. No. I did it a few times, because I had to, but I quickly promised myself I would never do it again.'

Soon, she was cleaning houses six, and sometimes seven, days a week. 'For the first couple of months,' she says, 'you are shattered constantly, you can barely walk home.' She would wake in the morning to find that her hands had doubled in size, swollen through overwork. 'They were in so much pain. I couldn't move them. I had to run them under cold water.'

The physicality proved a steep learning curve. It would take many months to get used to it, and it was gruelling. She missed her daughter dreadfully. 'You go through a lot, but you do make good money. And slowly, you get used to it, the physical labour, the job itself. But it's all you do. You work, you come home to your sofa bed in the shared house you live in, you shower, and you sleep. Just sleep. That's all you can do because you are so tired.'

But it was worth it. Soon she was making £2,000 a month, which, she points out, 'is okay from cleaning.'

Within three months, she was able to send for her daughter. The three of them continued to live in the shared house, the already cramped sofa bed even more cramped now, but in time they moved to their own small flat. Over the next few years, Yuliya thrived. Though her marriage would fail, she would buy her own place and start her own cleaning business, becoming an employer. Yuliya, who turned 40 in 2018, has secured British citizenship to make her and her daughter's future more solid. She is in a new relationship. She drives a gleaming white Mercedes, and dresses like Victoria Beckham.

Her 12-year-old daughter attends private school. Sending her daughter to private school, she tells me, means that her daughter will have a better start in life than she did, and that she won't have to be a cleaner herself. Yuliya is a success story.

'It's a good life now, I can say this,' she tells me. She employs between 35 and 40 women, all of them Bulgarian, all similarly educated and, like Yuliya, craving an honest job that allows them to earn a living. Much of what they earn is sent back to dependants at home. Yuliya likes her role, likes being the boss. 'But it's hard also.' I ask her why. She smiles ruefully. 'Working with people,' she says. 'It's never easy.'

Before she came to the UK, Yuliya had a certain image of British people. She says that all Bulgarians do. It's an image reliant upon stereotype and cultural signposts like James Bond and *Downton Abbey*, bowler hats and 'please' and 'thank you' and too much rain. When I ask her to describe this image to me, she looks off into the distance and smiles privately, pursing her lips. It takes several moments until she formulates an answer.

'In my country,' she begins, 'we imagine English people like this.' She raises her eyebrows in an attempt, I guess, to look aloof. She does it well. Then she lifts her espresso cup, and extends her little finger like somebody refined, a lady of the manor perhaps. Now she looks at me again. 'You know?' She bursts into laughter.

But this stereotype was dismantled quickly after her first few months here. British people, it turns out, are much like everybody else. For this she acknowledges the neighbourhood into which she settled, aware, she says, that she might have had very different experiences had she settled elsewhere. 'But this is all I know, and the people I meet, and work with, are so nice. Yes, some are fussy, and some are relaxed. Some really appreciate their cleaners, and some really don't, but mostly they are very nice people. They have high standards, they can be demanding, but they tell me this in a nice way, and when people tell you things in a nice way, you don't mind being told.'

She demurs when I ask whether cleaning houses has altered her impression of people, but what she will say is this:

'Some clients, even the very fussy and demanding ones, fail to maintain their own homes between our visits. They are not very good at cleaning up after themselves, and yet they still expect so very much of me and my staff. I don't mind this, I accept it, it's modern life, but the main thing I always say is: be nice. Be polite. Be careful how you say things to us, because we are people too; we have feelings. And we appreciate to know that you appreciate the work we are doing for you—especially if you really can't be bothered to do it for yourselves. So, please, just bear that in mind.'

She recalls one client she used to clean for, a heavy smoker who had been hospitalised several times due to his habit. They bonded over cigarettes. Every Wednesday morning when she arrived, he would have lined up for her a cup of tea and a Benson & Hedges. They would share their cigarettes across the kitchen table, and he would talk to her, asking her about her family, her progress here in the UK. This, she suggests, has been typical of people in the equable corner of London which she has made her home: they try to make a connection; they want to convey gratitude as a way to ameliorate their guilt.

'They have been so kind, mostly. They ask about me, like they care. The older clients especially. The older clients, they just want company a lot of the time. And in this neighbourhood, it's rare to bump into someone who is not like that—a nice person. I've always been given presents at Christmas—box of chocolates, a bonus.

This is important, you know, for my cleaners, too. It's not about what you get, it's about the gesture.'

Yuliya's new partner has a very different outlook. His London is another place altogether. He is a minicab driver, and, says Yuliya, 'his experience has not been like mine. He doesn't like the city. He says that all I see is middle-class people and upper-middle-class people. The people he drives do not treat him the way people treat me.'

How so, I ask? 'They are rude, they shout, they swear. When you drive on the streets here, the traffic is always so heavy, and the drivers are rude all the time, aggressive. It makes him stressed. But I don't see that, so I'm lucky. In people's homes, I see their better sides, I think.'

Due to her British citizenship, and what she suggests is the ongoing decline of her native country, Yuliya says that she is here to stay. 'I might go back one day, when I retire, if there is something to go back to, but otherwise I am happy here. This is my home.'

When I ask her why—given that she now speaks perfect English—she didn't pursue her original career ambition in finance and banking, she firmly shakes her head.

'No, no,' she says. 'In my time here, I've learned enough about people in England, and I don't want to be in competition with them. I could never go back to banking, not here.' I press her for a reason. 'People here, they are too ambitious. They put their careers first, beyond anybody else's. Not just their family members, but... How shall I put it? Being in competition in England would feel, I think, like not a very nice experience. I would be scared to be in competition with them. They want success for themselves too much, in a way that I think means they might not be very nice to each other. Does that make sense?'

She concedes that this is perhaps typical not just of London but any major international hub. But in Bulgaria, she insists, one wouldn't see this; in Bulgaria she would feel, perhaps not unsurprisingly, more at home. Setting up her own company here was part of laying more lasting foundations on her terms. She did it in part to appease her parents, who had once ran their own restaurant. Her mother hated the idea that her well-educated daughter had left their country in order to go to the UK to clean other people's mess. She wanted her to do well in her adopted country. Yuliya is now doing well. But it has been a struggle. At first she was taken advantage of, people trying to sell their services to her, acutely aware that she didn't have a perfect grasp of English, and aware, too, that she didn't know entirely how to operate in an English market. She was an easy target.

'So many people said that they could help me, that I needed their help to do what I needed to do. I lost several thousand pounds trying to advertise my company, trying to get it on the first page of Google search, things like this.' She shrugs. 'But I learned, you know?'

Very much in control now, Yuliya runs a tight ship. She tells me that she will only employ Bulgarians, 'because I know these people, they are like me.' Many are not conversant in English. She doesn't help them find homes, or to learn the language, because there are only so many hours in the day. 'But many come here with family members,' she says. 'They are not always alone.' All of them, like Yuliya several years previously, have left their homes in the hope of being able to start again, to live better. A great many have left what might be termed 'proper' jobs, higher status ones. Some see cleaning as merely a temporary measure, an injection of necessary cash. For others, cleaning might be all they have left.

'Bulgaria used to have eight or nine million people,' she tells me, 'but it's barely five million now. Only old people and young children are left, which means that perhaps as many as four million Bulgarians are living abroad. That is the only way our country sustains itself these days, surviving on money sent back from abroad.'

She reiterates her previous point, that cleaning here, in a metropolis like London, can be a good job. It can bring a measure of self-respect. 'I quite like the fact that we are helping people to have quality time, and less stress. Everybody employs cleaners today, it's seen as an essential thing. I think it's because people in England are forced to work long hours. They have a career, and even people without kids have no time for themselves any more. They know that they don't want to spend their weekends cleaning their homes after a hard week at work; they want to spend time with each other. I understand that. So it makes me feel good that we can help.'

Yuliya has a cleaner herself. 'Twice a week,' she says. 'And it's as important to me as it is to you. It makes us all feel less stressed, I think, coming home to a clean house.' She believes that you react less to mess when someone else is doing the cleaning up. 'If your kids make a mess in the house that you yourself have just cleaned, for hours and hours, then it stresses you out. But if your kids make a mess when it's the cleaner that has cleaned up, it somehow makes it easier. And that makes being a mum, a parent, easier. Just a little bit, you know? But it counts.'

***

What does it take to run your own cleaning company? To juggle the expectations of clients, and the temperaments of staff? According to Yuliya, much of her daily work involves a great deal of diplomacy. She is the facilitator who strives to please both employer and employee, ideally at the same time. She makes regular house visits to ensure that everything is running as it should, and each of her cleaners undergoes rigorous training before being let loose with a mop. They are taught how to clean, which products to use on different surfaces, whether the clothes that have been discarded on the floor should be folded and stored or put straight into the washing machine. Each employee, Yuliya explains, has their own idiosyncrasies. It is her job to learn them and to prepare her cleaners accordingly. 'The more we understand them, the better the relationship.'

Whenever clients aren't happy, Yuliya arrives to investigate why—to mediate, to moderate, to manage unreasonable expectation. Is the house too messy? Are the clients expecting a three-hour job to be done in two hours? Is the vacuum cleaner working properly, its suction hose sucking, the bag full?

Very often, clients want their houses cleaned in a highly particular way, and it is Yuliya's job to enlighten her cleaners, who, if they weren't particularly patient types before, are now. Yuliya tells me that homeowners can often be viewed as a whole, lumped together, many of us exhibiting similar behavioural quirks when it comes to the person who cleans our house. If something goes missing, for example, or if something is discovered to be broken, then it's the cleaner's fault, obviously, because whose else could it be? Not us, certainly, and not the children, who are precious and angelic and entirely innocent until proved otherwise. There isn't a week that goes by when one of her clients doesn't call her asking where the bread knife is, a payslip, a favourite shirt, a string of their dead grandmother's pearls. The salad bowl is chipped; the handle of a coffee cup has come away. The Xbox is suddenly malfunctioning. Where's the remote?

Guilty as charged. No judge, no jury.

'I very much believe it's a mental thing, yes,' Yuliya says. 'Something gets broken or lost, it must be the cleaner.'

Her employees are instructed to confess to any breakages immediately; to stop what they are doing and take a photograph of whatever it is they have destroyed—an IKEA saucer, a priceless heirloom—and send it to the office straight away. Yuliya will then inform the client while expressing the appropriate apologies, and offer to pay for the damages.

But more often than not, she insists, the cleaner is not at fault.

'We reach for that assumption because it is the easiest one to reach for,' she says, 'but a lot of the times the girls have nothing to do with it.'

She offers an example. One of her team was accused of stealing a video camera. 'My girl, she was in tears. She swore that she hadn't taken it, would never do anything like that. She was honest, trustworthy.'

The client was furious; the video camera was worth hundreds of pounds. The client summarily sacked the cleaner. She sank into a depression, and was reluctant to continue her work lest she find herself accused of something else she hadn't done. Then, a few days later, Yuliya received an email—an apology. The video camera was found. 'It had been in a cupboard somewhere.'

It was pleasing that the client had corrected their mistake, but too late. The damage had been done. Yuliya no longer wanted them on her books, and a mutually fruitful relationship was severed.

'They were not very nice to us, but I am glad that they got in touch. At least I knew that my girl hadn't done anything wrong.'

Yuliya has been in the UK for 12 years. She has acclimatised, and flourished. But she remains very much Bulgarian. Her new partner is Bulgarian, as is her social circle. And though she no longer believes that all British people are ungainly caricatures as created by Julian Fellowes and Richard Curtis, she still feels slightly distanced from them.

'I know some Bulgarians who came here as cleaners but who are now married to English men and are very happy, and integrated,' she says, 'but for me, culturally, it is still hard. I have tried many times going out with English people, trying to make jokes with them, and have relationships. But it's difficult. We laugh at different things, I think. Our jokes are different, our humour. We probably see life a little differently, too. I do like it here, and it has become home for me, and for my daughter—my daughter is British—but for me I will always feel different, and separate. But that's okay. It's okay.'

She finishes her espresso, and places both hands flat on the table between us, all business. Speaking of which, she has to go. Time is money. 'It's life, you know?' she says, standing up, brushing herself down. 'Not perfect, but you get on with it.'

2. The Actress

When someone cleans for a living, it can mean that they have given up on their life's ambition. In many cases, it's merely a necessary stopgap, the only thing available in the short-term; grunt work that rarely shines on a CV. This temporary arrangement can often drag on, lumbering towards permanency. Nevertheless, those that do it spend their working hours dreaming they are elsewhere, far away, doing something better.

'English people are not going to clean their own toilets, are they?' Rosi, a Spanish woman, says, her tone one of withering disbelief. 'I love English people, I do. But, no, they wouldn't do that. But then it's the same in our country: it's the immigrants that do certain jobs. It's just that here, in the UK, we are the immigrants.'

It's a Saturday afternoon on London's South Bank, in late 2018, when I first meet Rosi. She is late by at least a couple of hours, having got caught up—and lost all track of time—on a march to protest against Brexit alongside hundreds and thousands of people. She is emotional when she arrives, and speaks hopefully about people power. 'This is the second march I am going on,' she tells me. 'Is the same in my country. The Basque region wants to separate. No. We are stronger together.'

Rosi is 47 years old, her straw blonde hair pulled up tight into a high ponytail. She is smart and fashionable, but Spanish fashionable rather than British. Despite having lived in Tooting for the past seven years, she doesn't look, or sound, particularly anglicised.

'I buy all my clothes when I'm back in Madrid,' she says. 'Cheaper.'

When I ask if she is married, whether she has children, she takes a deep breath. She shakes her head swiftly once, as if the topic causes her discomfort, a stream of melancholy she wishes to dam. Back at home, she was an amateur actress, who hoped, one day, to turn professional. 'You see, I always loved the literature, theatre, the arts,' she says. At school and university, she was part of drama groups that put on plays; sometimes, but not always, she took the lead. She clamps a hand to her forehead, laughing. 'But this is all many, many years ago!'

Perhaps it is, and perhaps the ambition was never realised, but her dramatic instincts remain. She speaks English in a vivid accent that karate chops consonants. Everything she says comes with much gesticulation: her arms flail, and her face takes on myriad expressions—mouth formed into an 'O' to express shock, eyebrows a pronounced 'V' for anger.

'I hope to return to it soon, the stage,' she adds. 'And I tell you about this later, afterwards. But not yet.' She smiles, and winks, wanting to pique my interest, while building a narrative arc.

After university, she became an interior designer. Although in a competitive market in Madrid, for a while Rosi, eager and driven, thrived. But her career didn't progress as she might have liked. Life became complicated, the details of which she will not convey to a stranger, no matter how much she likes to talk. There is a thin line between sharing and over-sharing, and Rosi walks on just the right side of it.

At the age of 40, she felt that life was over for her in Spain. She came to London.

'Once you are 40 there, is difficult.' She tells me that many industries strictly adhere to this assumption: young people power and rejuvenate the workforce, not the middle-aged. 'After 40 you are, like, finished.' She shrugs. 'Is funny. You study for your degree, you finish your degree, you are very employable, but there is not enough work. For me, too, as an interior designer, not enough work. You get older, so you go somewhere else, and try your luck there. Then, after a while, a few years maybe, you want to go back. Many people—not me, perhaps, but many people—they go back home with this new experience that can help them with their jobs, their careers. But—no. Now Spain says you are too old.'

The original plan had been to make a name for herself here in the UK, to establish her reputation. There are many Spaniards living in London. She could have designed their rooms and they would have recommended her to friends and family back home.

But London is full of interior designers, and Rosi soon found herself crowded out. Her English, back then, was minimal, her accent even stronger. This, she believes, held her back.

'When you speak English, is easier. I try to become fluent, but when you are old, learning a language is difficult.' It wasn't just a question of fluency, however. 'Is too competitive here, more so even than in Spain.'

For a time, she worked in what she calls the 'refurbishment industry,' alongside builders. She would paint rooms in houses, and repair them, make them pretty and oversee their feng shui. But such jobs were few and far between. Meanwhile, she had bills to pay. 'And so guess what? I become cleaner!' She shrugs again now and her shoulders communicate an entire novel's worth of emotions: sadness, disappointment, resignation, a whiff of existential despair.

'In your life, you will always have to do jobs you never thought you would do. This makes you more human, I think. So I have to see this as an opportunity for growth.'

Even now, I ask her, seven years on? She nods her head. 'Yes! I will learn English properly—I will!—and I will grow.'

Cleaning was supposed to be short-term only. But the past seven years give lie to this. She cleaned—offices, houses—then offered her services as a nanny. 'You do what you can to survive.' She tried to integrate, to create new social circles, but to her the British seemed standoffish, unfriendly—suspicious, even. Those she did socialise with were almost exclusively Spanish, and in much the same circumstances as her. Among her number there were no interior designers.

'But is okay,' she says. 'The people I meet are nice. And anyway, there is little time to have fun. If you want to make money in this city, then you have to work all the time. And I work all the time.'

Before long, she was working two jobs, then a third. She started cleaning offices at 3am, which enabled her to finish at dawn so that she could be cleaning her first private house by 7am. She would walk sundry children to school in a haze of fatigue, then return to the house to sleepwalk through the ironing while watching *A Place in the Sun* on TV, which all too often featured British couples trying to leave Rosi's adopted country in favour of her native one.

Frequently, she was sleeping only a couple of hours a night, rest being subservient to the need to earn a living.

She returned home less and less, and grew more roots here. Her friends, almost all Spanish and South American, became her family, and over time they began to meet up once a week to eat and laugh and drink, and where they could share horror stories until they became anecdotes. In this way, their frustrations dissolved. In her position, she says, you don't want your horror stories to fester.

She offers an example. 'People in offices, they don't care so much what you are doing, so you don't have to work quite so hard as you do in people's homes. You don't have to polish quite so much, you know? But then sometimes they behave more badly in the offices, and this I don't understand.'

Her eyebrows assuming their 'V' position, she continues. Once, she says, she had been cleaning an office block all morning, and was about to stop for lunch when her boss asked whether she could address a somewhat urgent manner in one of the unisex toilets. Rosi looked up at the clock, which ticked in sync with her stomach's grumblings, but nodded, and wheeled her bucket and mop over to the WC.

'Someone made poop on the floor,' she says. 'Right there on the floor, in the middle of everything, between toilet and sink.' She had been looking forward to her sandwich, but in an instant, her appetite vanished. Why did someone 'poop' on the floor? 'Because they can,' is the only answer she can come up with. 'And because no one will know who did it. Perhaps because at the office, they care less? Because nobody would make poop on the floor at home, I am thinking.'

Of course, an employee may have been leaving an angry message about their work. What was certain was that Rosi was the only one left with a shit job.

She was livid at the time, but by that Friday night the episode had morphed into something so hilarious, among her friends, that it prompted howls of laughter, and tears to the eyes. How else to cope otherwise? At the time, she'd felt like quitting. 'Because this is my life: cleaning shit from the floor. Unbelievable, right?'

But Rosi has a plan, one that she hopes will revive the woman she once was.

She wants to start acting again, to establish a community theatre group among her peers. They will meet once a week with a view to putting on plays whose themes allow them to express what it's like to be cleaners in a foreign city, far from home. And, she adds, 'to get it all out of our system, you know?'

She is under few illusions. She knows that organising such a group might prove difficult, and not all of them will be quite as committed as Rosi. But, for her, this could be a wonderful thing. Such a group, she suggests, will help everyone to overcome the feelings of disassociation and alienation they often experience. It will bring them closer and may profoundly strengthen their bonds.

'When you are separated from people you love, as we are, then to be able to perform theatrical pieces together—well, it brings you together like a family, a new family. Is therapy through drama; art therapy.'

In this way, Rosi is refusing to allow her old self to die. She may no longer be the young, idealistic Spaniard who thought she might act for a living, perhaps following in the footsteps of Penélope Cruz or Maribel Verdú, and nor is she an interior designer who travels the world at the behest of A-list clients. Circumstance has forced her down other routes, while the casual cruelties of capitalism have kept her there, stuck in a rut.

But, she says, there is more to someone than the work they do, just as the work we do shouldn't change the people we fundamentally are. 'Not in here, the heart. You know?'

As she continues to express herself in clattering consonants, constantly apologising for any grammatical mistakes, while laughing through fingers pressed to her mouth, Rosi remains the person she always was: bright, sunny and optimistic, driven. She avers that, even at the advanced Spanish age of 47, she is still a person of worth, fully three-dimensional, with hidden depths and layers, and with so much to offer, and to give.

'I tell you why I came to London, yes?' she says, the 'y' in 'yes' a hard 'j.' 'I came to London because I want for opportunities, opportunities to do the things I cannot do in my own country. Is difficult here, for sure, but this is where I started my personal growth.

'Spain,' she says, 'gave me my roots. But London has given me my wings.'

When I catch up with Rosi a year later, she has turned some of her dreams into reality. As a qualified Cognitive Behavioural Therapy and Neurolinguistic Programming teacher, she now runs workshops that help people deal with their emotions through movement, a style of dance where the expression of inner feelings is more important than rhythm. It's a format inspired by the Brazilian theatre practitioner Augusto Boal, founder of the Theatre of the Oppressed, which uses theatre as a tool for social change.

Because she still struggles in English, Rosi works primarily with Spanish-speaking immigrants, most of whom, like her, live permanently in London.

'Some people come occasionally, others come all the time,' she explains. 'They come because they want to talk in a safe environment, without being judged. And here, in my classes, they are able to open up, and talk freely. You know, London is a great city, there is a lot to do always, but many people, they are still lonely, so they come to the group as a way to connect with others, to feel like they are part of something. And many people, they make friendships that go beyond the workshops.'

Boal developed these techniques to help individuals express their emotions without using words, and so Rosi guides her students into creating images and shapes with their bodies. 'The purpose,' she says, 'is to assist with emotional intelligence, so that they can let out their feelings. We have so many emotions, all

3. Slave Labour

Those who get into cleaning don't always do so willingly, but by necessity and even force. Some are modern day slaves, tricked and trafficked into London under false pretences, their autonomy as vanished as their identities. Such stories are as tragic as they are abundant.

Amirah has been cleaning for much of her adult life. She is 41 years old but, despite experiencing severe hardship, looks no older than 25. She is small and compact, like a child. Her angelic, perfectly round face is framed within a hijab. She blinks languidly like a Disney doe, but her story is a grim modern tale.

Amirah comes from a small town in Indonesia, four hours from the capital Jakarta. While she may have entertained the dreams and ambitions typical of any teenager, her reality had little space for flights of fancy. 'I'm not really educated, you see,' she tells me, falteringly, 'so I had to work.'

She had finished primary school with hopes of going on to secondary school like others in her neighbourhood, but instead had to leave to help her mother look after her younger siblings. So she sought employment. Her village had few jobs and poor prospects. Consequently, aged 15, she was sent to Saudi Arabia as a domestic worker. The work there was long and gruelling; she was not treated fairly or well. She doesn't like to talk about her time in Saudi Arabia. Aged 21, she returned home to be told by her mother that it was time to marry and have a family.

Frowning, she tells me: 'It was not really a happy situation, my marriage.' She had two children, both of them girls. The paucity of available work, for both her and her new husband, put further strain on a marriage that was already close to breaking point. 'I had so many loans, mostly for everyday living,' she says. 'It was very difficult. I needed to work. I needed to make money.'

She signed up to an agency that sent domestic cleaners around the world. Like so many of her countrywomen, she would work elsewhere, anywhere, and send her salary back. She didn't want to return to Saudi, didn't want a repeat of her teenage experiences, and elected instead to travel to either the US, or perhaps the UK. She had been told that there was money to make in these countries, and the fact that she could just about get by in English made her readily employable. She had little idea of how to apply for such a job, but this is why the agency existed—for a fee it assisted with the application process, the paperwork. The agency, in Jakarta, would arrange everything: a new passport, and a visa that allowed Amirah to work as a cleaner in a foreign embassy, but nowhere else. This was fine by her; why would she look elsewhere? Foreign embassy work was desirable, above board. It came with a certain respect. She would have somewhere to live, and a uniform. She would be paid well.

Amirah was surprised that the agency went about preparing her documents with the stealth of a secret organisation. She was to tell no one where she was going, for instance, and wouldn't herself know when she was leaving until days beforehand. It wasn't easy passing through security checks at international airports, even when you were destined for embassy work. She would have to... not lie, exactly, but come up with another, plausible, reason. Just in case. She was to say that she was seeing family members. 'But my family members are all here in Indonesia,' she thought to herself. She had no concept of the UK, her preferred location. She knew that London was the capital, and that she wanted to go there. Tell them London, she was told. The prospect made her nervous. She was sick to the stomach at the prospect. She prayed.

It took months for the passport to arrive, then months more for a visa. By this time, she was in even more debt. The agency was a four-hour round trip from her home. Every trip exhausted her. She tried to focus on the benefits that were to come. She had been told that she could earn as much as £500 a month as a live-in maid in London. Food would be provided. This would leave her with plenty to send home to her family.

'You need to be efficient, you need to be polite, you need to be good at your job.' She was repeatedly told this mantra until she fell asleep reciting it. 'You will be working for a diplomat,' they said to her. 'You will need to be discreet.'

Amirah still didn't fully understand what was expected of her, or where she was going. Once again, she was told to say that she would be visiting family, and staying with them for a period of time. She could tell them that she was looking forward to sightseeing: Big Ben, Buckingham Palace, the Tower of London. Harrods and Selfridges. Amirah wanted to know how easy it would be to fool customs officers. 'It will be no problem; you will be fine,' they told her. She tried to believe them, but she had nightmares.

At least she wasn't travelling alone. She would be flying with a friend, also destined for some kind of foreign embassy cleaning work in the capital. The foreign embassy had yet to be specified. No matter. The day came, she said goodbye to her daughters, her husband, her mother, and she left.

Almost immediately things went wrong.

'My friend was very beautiful,' Amirah says. 'So when we were showing our passports and they started to ask us questions, they didn't believe us. They thought we were travelling to the UK to become sex workers. I had to tell them that, no, no we were not. We were going to see family.' They were asked where, precisely, in the capital her family was based. Amirah began to panic. In

retelling it now, her eyes grow wide. Her mouth falls open. '...
London,' I told them. 'I said we were to be collected at the airport.
We were looking forward to our... our holiday.'

Amirah arrived into London on 20th July 2009. Hers was one of
the first planes to touch down at Heathrow that morning, and she
made it through passport control, nervous and exhausted but
safe, at 7am. She and her friend walked tentatively into Arrivals
clutching their luggage, looking eagerly out for the person from
the agency who was coming to collect them. They had no name,
no phone number.

'We were hungry, and very tired,' she says.

They took their suitcases to some seats, and sat down. They
waited an hour, then two. After four hours, still nobody had come.
They were frantic by now, albeit silently, fearful of showing their
panic lest they attract unwanted attention. What were they
supposed to do? One of the world's major cities was on their
doorstep, but they had no money, no idea where to go. Their
English was rudimentary.

The man from the agency did eventually arrive, six hours late,
with no explanation, no apology. Refusing to buy them food, he
impatiently bade them to follow him to his car. He had only paid
for half an hour; parking is expensive at Heathrow. The car was
large, and boxy. It smelled inside like a fight had taken place
between pine air freshener and cigarettes, with the cigarettes

claiming victory. The man wasn't particularly talkative. He smoked. Music murmured in the background from speakers low in the door panel. Amirah and her friend watched as the grey environs of west London gave way, slowly, to colour, to open green spaces, to skyscrapers. The sun shone and the tarmac below them raced by. London! They had made it. Amirah tried to summon up some excitement, but all she felt was a wariness that gnawed at her bones.

Her destination, she believed now, was the Saudi embassy. She could speak Arabic from her time in Saudi Arabia as a teenager. She had no idea where the embassy was, and so when they pulled up at a house which she only later learned was in an area called East Acton, she could not know that this was nothing at all to do with the embassy in Mayfair. All she saw was a drab, large house on a quiet suburban street. The family was Arabic, of this she was sure, but otherwise their full identities would remain deliberately concealed.

She was welcomed, without a smile, at the front door by the lady of the house. Back in the car, her driver took off, taking her beautiful Indonesian friend elsewhere. She would not see her again. The lady of the house was officious, businesslike, in her late thirties, perhaps early forties. She walked her through the house, and up the stairs, to show her her room which, Amirah saw, doubled as the cleaning closet. Her bed was located underneath the boiler which, she would discover, clanked and grumbled throughout the night. There was no cupboard, no chest of drawers. No window. She placed her bag down, then followed the lady back downstairs. Her work was about to begin.

'She told me to clean the kitchen, to take everything out of the drawers and cupboards, and to clean everything with chemicals.' Amirah was tired—she hadn't slept on the plane—but began working straight away, intent on making a good impression. The lady of the house did not retreat, but rather, arms folded against her chest, watched her toil. She proved a hard task master, finding fault in everything Amirah did. 'Every second, it seemed like, she shouts at me.'

In this way, a regular working relationship was instantaneously established. 'I work from seven in the morning to the middle of the night. If they have a visitor, then I have to stay awake until they have finished, sometimes three or four o'clock in the morning. Then I have to get up again a few hours later to make breakfast for the children. All I did was clean, all day, most of the night. And every second, every moment it seemed, she shouts at me, always shouting.'

Amirah's job was to look after the house: to clean it daily to a high specification; to look after the children. There were four children, from toddler to teenage. She would cook for all the family, throughout the day, eating her own food in the kitchen, on the doormat.

When she says the word doormat, I assume there has been some confusion. I ask her to repeat it. 'The doormat?' I say. She nods her head.

'Yes. By the door, on the floor.'

She had to eat sitting on the floor? But why?

This time she shakes her head. 'I don't know. She didn't want me to eat at the table.'

Mirroring their mother, the children treated Amirah as a serf, a lower caste person who was not quite as human as they were, undeserving of empathy. 'The children called me names, and used to taunt me. They would tell their mother that I beat them. I never beat them, I never touched them. I was scared of them.'

Each night, Amirah cried herself to sleep. She prayed to God. 'Oh God, oh God, please just give me one day of relief. Let the lady not shout at me. I prayed because I was worried. I worried all night what would happen the next day. It was like the movies, a horror movie, a beast waiting for you, around the corner.'

She became an insomniac. She lost weight, and felt highly stressed and anxious. She recounts this with some discomfort, as we sit in a canteen. She sips from a cup of coffee as a young boy, her son, sits in her lap, playing with his mother's phone. Amirah lowers her voice to something just above a whisper. 'You know when you are feeling depression, and you are thinking [of doing] something bad?' she says to me. 'That's what I was thinking.' She grimaces. 'But then I had to think of my kids back home in Indonesia. If I did something... bad to myself, then what happens to my kids? I am their provider. I need to support them.'

At home, her daughters were initially being looked after by her mother, but then her ex-husband took them in. 'It was not a good situation,' she says.

She focused instead on the money that she was supposed to be earning: £500 a week went a long way in Indonesia. 'Yes,' she says, 'but I didn't get paid. They didn't pay me.'

For the duration of her stay in East Acton, Amirah was told not to go out. When the rubbish bins in the kitchen were full, she could not take them out to the big bins outside until dark. If anyone were to talk to her, she was instructed not to talk back. Later, she would learn that in the house next door there was also a cleaner, also probably from south east Asia. She was told not to have any contact with this woman, not even to glance in her direction. 'The lady of the house would watch me from the window,' she says. 'I had to do a lot of gardening, and sometimes the other cleaner was in the next door garden, over the fence.'

The other cleaner seemed chatty, and wanted to engage in conversation. But if Amirah so much as raised her head, a top floor window would fly open, and the lady of the house would scream at her to get back inside. Amirah knew well enough to retreat. She lived in a state of terror. She only summoned up the strength to enquire about her pay four full months into her stay there.

'I said, can I have my salary please? And they said, next week, next week, next week.'

At this point in our conversation, Amirah breaks down and cries. It is horrible to watch. Her son looks briefly up at her, before the game recaptures his gaze. She brings a hand to both eyes to rub away the tears.

'Mental abuse,' she tells me, 'it's the same as physical abuse. Physical abuse, you get hurt. But mentally, you know. You get hurt as well. And it's still there. It still hurts.'

One afternoon, while she was gardening, the family went out. She was almost never home alone, and so allowed herself the novelty of relaxing, slightly. The neighbour's cleaner saw her, and went out to talk. She was friendly. 'Where are you from?' she asked. Amirah told her. 'I'm from Indonesia, too!' the other said. They began to talk, furtively, in fevered whispers. The woman asked her how long she had been in the house. Five months, Amirah told her. 'Five months! But I've hardly seen you!' Amirah did her best to describe her working conditions, and that she hadn't yet been paid. The woman became agitated, and told her that Amirah was being exploited, that she should change employer, that in this country she had rights. 'You should leave: escape!'

'I told her I was too afraid. I told her that because I only had a visa to work for a diplomat, I couldn't change jobs. Also, where would I go? So it was impossible for me. But this woman, she insisted.'

A window upstairs opened. One of the sons must have returned. He shouted at her, called her names. Amirah ran inside, cowed, and resumed her work.

One evening, the family had guests. The dinner went on late, long after midnight. They were loud and disruptive. The younger children were woken from sleep and began crying. Amirah tended to them. She eventually settled the youngest with a bottle of warmed milk. By the time she went back down to the kitchen it was 4am. Exhausted, she placed the empty bottle in the sink and went to bed. She was asleep before her head hit the pillow.

Less than three hours later, the alarm clock went off. Her uniform was still wet from its wash the night before. Amirah was not allowed to wear her own clothes, but nor was she allowed to wash her uniform in one of the house's several washing machines. Instead, she had had to clean it by hand, and then hang it in the bathroom to dry. But it was cold and damp in the bathroom, and now it was wintertime; drying was taking longer.

So Amirah wore her normal clothes. The lady of the house wasn't happy. She raised her voice, berating her for flouting the rules. A moment later, she spotted the baby's bottle on its side in the sink. Now she became shrill. 'What did I tell you!' she screamed. 'You are never allowed to go to bed until you have finished cleaning everything, everything! So what is this?' Her finger pointed to the sink's sole inhabitant, an empty bottle of milk that Amirah had used the night before to calm the lady's daughter.

Amirah needed to be punished. She was instructed to clean the entire kitchen, every implement, every surface, with bleach. The lady withheld the rubber gloves.

Several hours later, Amirah's hands were cracked and bleeding, fizzing with pain. She wanted to go upstairs to her bathroom to run them under cold water, but the children had arrived back from school. There was homework to assist with, dinner to prepare.

Dark thoughts descended again. She had to remind herself of her daughters, thousands of miles away, wondering what had happened to their mother, why she had fallen so silent, where all of the promised money was.

The cleaner next door was enterprising. She knew how to act without being seen, under the cover of night if necessary, or tree shade in daytime. One afternoon, while gardening, she managed to pass a £20 note through the separating fence to Amirah undetected. She had it all planned out. She told Amirah to wait until the family was out, then to go into the lady of the house's bedroom, and root through her drawers until she found her passport, which had been confiscated upon Amirah's arrival and not returned. The moment she had her passport, she should pack her bag and run. But where? Amirah wanted to know. She gave her the address of somewhere in London, a place called Camberwell. 'Cam-ber-well.' There would be help here.

Amirah was terrified. But she was also desperate. It was three o'clock on a Monday afternoon. She remembers it like it was yesterday. 'A very cold winter's day,' she tells me. 'And I didn't have a jacket. I was very much relieved to find my passport, but I left everything else. I didn't have time. And I didn't know where I was going.'

Closing the front door behind her for what she hoped would be the last time, she ran down the street she had lived on for the past five months. Everything was new to her. She had seen none of it before. She turned a corner, and kept running. Her panic beat a rhythm to match her heart, which felt swollen, high up in her throat. Up ahead she saw an elderly couple putting shopping from a supermarket trolley into the boot of a car. She stopped to ask them, in broken English, where the train station was, but as they began to give her directions, she let out a howl and burst into tears.

'I told them the truth, that I had escaped from my employer and that I didn't know where I was.' The couple listened with sympathy, and told her that she was right to flee. They offered to drive her to the train station, then gave her £10 for a ticket. She now had a total of £30 to fund her escape.

The journey by car took them past her employer's house. Amirah, in the back seat, cowered down, trembling with fear. At the station, she thanked the couple profusely, then tried to work out where she was, where she needed to go. How to buy a ticket.

Confusingly, the train map branched out into several directions. She had been told to look out for Victoria. At Victoria she would have to change, but she wasn't entirely sure what 'change' might mean here. Change what?

Half an hour later, she got out at Victoria station, the biggest thing she had seen since Heathrow. Only there were even more people, so many people. The concourse teemed, a riot of colour and chaos. What to do? She found it difficult to focus her eyes. She remembered what the cleaner next door had told her, mentioning an underground train and a bus. But where was this underground? She stumbled out into the forecourt, and saw a queue of squat black cars: taxis. She approached one, and fished out the address she had been given for the help that was waiting for her in the place called Cam-ber-well.

The driver nodded once. 'Yep, I can take you,' he told her. She asked him how much, and he replied. What she understood was '50.' 'Fifty!' she cried in disbelief. She didn't have 50. No, no, he said patiently. Fifteen. One, five. She looked at the notes balled up in her hand, and knew that she had enough. He took her south of the river, to SE5.

In Camberwell, Southwark Community Action Networks is a charity for refugees. It confirmed to her that her visa was particularly restrictive and that she would find it difficult to get a new job. 'If I didn't work in a diplomat's house, then I couldn't work anywhere,' she says. Her only other option was cash-in-hand work, but even in a good economy, this proved difficult. One tends not to find live-in domestic work without the necessary papers. With the charity's help, she took her case to the Home Office.

In the meantime, she followed advice and advertised on Gumtree: Domestic Cleaner for Hire. Gumtree can sometimes be like a rowdy pub at closing time: anything can happen, much of it off script, occasionally unpleasant. She started to receive a lot of texts on her new mobile phone, people saying they wanted her services, but not always restricted to cleaning. One man was quite upfront about his intentions when he texted her. 'I do want a cleaner,' he wrote, 'but also a girlfriend. You, perhaps?' It says a lot about Amirah's general demeanour that she politely declined his offer, not wanting to cause offence.

'I didn't know,' she says. 'Is this what England is like?'

There were other responses, more normal ones. She turned up for interviews, and they seemed to go well. She made a good impression. She had been instructed, by staff at the charity, to tell the truth, that she didn't have papers right now, but that her case was being processed by the Home Office. But for prospective employers, this wasn't enough. A job eluded her.

'I got very upset, and so I am just crying and crying, desperate to get a job,' she says. One day, she found herself on a bus far from Camberwell after yet another unsuccessful interview, and cried all the way to the last stop. She apologised to the driver, who consoled her. She tumbled out of the bus. 'I had no idea where I was. It took me hours to get back.'

But eventually she did get work, in the outer corridors of London where it becomes leafier and more breathable, for an Iraqi family that did pay her, but that required her services seven days a week. The work was fair but relentless. That didn't matter. At last she was being paid. At last she could send money back. Her daughters were grateful, her ex-husband relieved.

Several years have elapsed since Amirah stopped working for the Iraqi family. She is currently waiting for a visa that will allow her reasonable grounds to continue to remain. This is because the Home Office have agreed that she has been a victim of trafficking into the country. She tries on a cautious smile, as if for size. 'So I may be permitted to stay.' She lives in temporary accommodation under the flight path in west London, alongside fellow asylum seekers.

She is unable to work for the time being, and has been told not to seek cash-in-hand jobs. She receives £73 a week from the government, which allows her to provide for her son, if not quite for her daughters back home in Indonesia.

Her son is five years old. He looks small, and thin, for his age. I ask if she is married, perhaps hoping that she will offer some small good fortune in what is otherwise a very sad story. No, she says. She isn't.

'His daddy left when my son was two months old.'

So you are alone? 'Yes.'

She begins quietly to cry. 'When you don't have anything, when you are just waiting and waiting, this means that you are worrying all the time.' She nods her head to further affirm her point. 'I am on antidepressant medication. I am worried that my claim might be refused, because what then?'

She tells me that going home would be problematical. She points to her young son, born out of wedlock, without a father. 'Indonesia is a Muslim country. If I go back to my country with my son and I am not married, it is a difficult situation. I would be isolated. There will be stigma on me. My daughters, they don't know that I have a child here. If I tell them, they will probably forget me.'

She still speaks regularly to her girls, but only when her son is asleep. She cannot let them know that he exists, so their relationship glides along on lies. Both daughters want to go to university. 'They want a better life than me.' For this they need money, but Amirah is not in a position to send money back. She had thought that cleaning in a country as liberal as Britain would allow her to make a life for herself. She had been looking forward to making money, paying tax, sending money home, then following the money and resuming her life in Asia. She thought that when she did return to Indonesia, she could start studying again, to make something of herself. But it hasn't worked out that way. So she is stuck here.

But even if she did go back, what then? 'This is a situation I worry about every day,' she says. 'This country has been kind to me. I have somewhere to stay now, but it's not home, and so I'm not really comfortable about my life. I was trafficked here, but I have been here a long time, almost 10 years. I have,' she says, pointing to her son, 'him now.'

Despite her situation, she likes London. She senses that it is fundamentally democratic, and fair. 'Things here seem, you know, real, like anything can happen. You can feel that everyone here is equal, whether you are rich or poor, domestic worker or doctor. In my own country, I would feel like a stranger now. When you are poor there, you have low status. No one looks at you, no one talks to you. They only recognise you as a person if you are rich, if you have money. If I go home, my life would only be trouble, not just for me, but my kids, my family. My daughters would have trouble getting married if it becomes known that I had a son like this, because no family would want to marry into a family like mine. Stigma, you understand? You are judged a lot for this in my country, but less here, I think.'

She is trying to remain optimistic. Securing a visa that would allow her discretionary leave to remain means that she would be able to work legally. This is something she craves very much indeed. She says she wants to contribute to the country that has looked after her, that has saved her. I ask whether she would return to domestic work, the only work she has ever known.

'I don't think so,' she tells me, 'no. There are very bad memories for me in cleaning, you see.'

Instead, she thinks she might like to work with young children. A nanny, perhaps. She wants to improve her English, to return to education. As middle age beckons, she would like to make something of herself. So far, her life hasn't worked out the way she would have wanted, but she believes that if she does secure a visa, then she may have a second chance.

'I would like to do something else with my life now,' she says. 'I would like to start again.'

4. Midlife Crisis

Where some people are forced into a world of servitude, others select it when other areas of their life have shut down. Michele, for example, didn't become a cleaner until her late forties, after a midlife crisis conspired to tip her into a new—and wholly unexpected—role.

'It was 2010, and I was 49,' she says. 'I had kids, a husband, a life—and then something went wrong with me.'

Panic and anxiety attacks sporadically crashed into her life. She would self-medicate with sedatives. Valium worked for a while until it didn't. Then it would only work if she washed down the pills with alcohol. 'A couple of hits a vodka with 5 mg of Valium is pretty fantastic, you know?' She laughs out loud. 'I became this kind of weird Judy Garland person.'

Michele is a former journalist. She is from New York but has lived in London for three decades. When the writing commissions dried up, she needed to reinvent herself. Reinvention is difficult, and she struggled. The pills numbed her to an extent, but then took over her life. She ended up in rehab, and returned some time later to her family—the family that she had left—to tell them that she was well now. But they had moved on, and, for a time at least, she was no longer welcome among them.

'I was, like: "Ri-ight, okay. What do I do now?"'

She moved out of their shared home and into a small flat in East London. Now in her mid-fifties, she was living alone, a blank slate. This was more of a stuttering halt than a fresh start. She became, to all intents and purposes, agoraphobic, the outside world having turned hostile on her. Worse, she was forced to sign on the dole.

'Do you know how horrible it is to be on the dole?' she asks. 'Horrible, horrible. I decided that I would do anything to avoid being on the dole ever again. So I turned to cleaning.'

Though she faced the unavoidable problem of actually getting from her flat to the house that needed cleaning, once she was in it, she was inside again. Safe. 'Agoraphobics do like to be within four walls,' she says. 'And most of the time the homes were empty, or the people stayed out of my way while I was fixing up their stuff. It seemed the best option, and of course they paid me to clean, so that was pretty much it for me. I thought to myself: "Okay, this is what I'll do."'

To a former newspaper and magazine writer, cleaning was a severe demotion. She had been born in the US to a Canadian father educated in England and a mother from Liverpool. Aged 24, she moved to the UK and worked as a journalist in the booming music business of the 1980s and 90s. She could still remember the parties she attended. The canapés, the champagne, the excess. The trips around the world to interview the rich and famous. In the new millennium new technology sucker-punched the business and pop writers now staggered across a once verdant landscape like members of the living dead. Michele had to diversify. She became a press officer briefly, then a tour manager for a US folk singer-songwriter. Then, eventually, she ran out of road, and started cleaning houses.

'And now I was strictly low status. But, hey, to the people I cleaned for at least, I was unusual, and I suppose I liked that. They heard me talk, and I wasn't talking in an eastern European accent. I smiled a lot. In other words, I didn't look like a typical cleaner, whatever a typical cleaner might look like.'

Initially, she signed up with a local agency where she had been told that one doesn't just 'become' a cleaner. Training was required, even for someone with her life skills. 'So I had to do a test run to see whether I was worthy of the gig. Two hours, and for that I got paid two quid. If, at the end of those two hours, they said I wasn't good enough, then at least I could walk away with the two quid, right?'

She may have left the US a long time ago, but Michele still talks like a New Yorker.

The 'low status' tag didn't particularly bother her. She had learned a lot about status in rehab. Life was starting again, and if it was to be from the bottom up, then so be it. Whenever she had been invited to dinner parties in the past, her various jobs always prompted conversations. She was interesting to talk to, had lots of stories and a quick wit. But now when she attended them—and she points out that dinner party invites don't come her way very much any more—her new career proved a conversation starter for all the wrong reasons.

'I knew it was demeaning, but then I'd accepted that. But the reaction from other people made me realise just how much we invest in this stuff. It's all about what we do, who we are. I'm a journalist; I'm a psychologist; whatever. People judge you accordingly. When you say to people you don't really know that you are a cleaner, it freaks them out. They don't understand; they don't even get why you are there in the first place. They have questions: why are you a cleaner? Yes, but why?'

She learned that one's profession is a bridge to the conversational flow: journalist, fine; ambulance driver, fascinating. But if your job is a menial one, the drawbridge is raised. Conversation stops. Awkwardness arrives.

'People asked if this was just a stopgap for me, and I would answer: "Mate, I'm in my fifties, I've given up. This is what I do now. I clean!"'

She never quite felt the sense of devastation that people expected her to feel. She made her own hours, and rarely more than three houses a day. 'I was never going to become Cleaner of the Month. Cleaner of the Month would work for 10 to 12 hours a day; I'd work no more than five or six. I needed Income Support to top up my pay. That's their present to you, by the way—the government. Income Support for not being on the dole. I was grateful for it.'

Michele was confident that she would never go back to writing again. 'Proper' work was now beyond her, as was her family, who were still functioning without her. She cleaned houses because it was the only thing she could do, and if she took an interest in her clients, a writerly interest, it was cursory and never spiced with much curiosity. That sense of journalistic intrigue—nosiness by any other name—had long since withered.

But the job was hardly dull.

'Stepping into beautiful homes was always a little disconcerting. It was like stepping into a show home, everything in its place, and I was like: what on earth am I supposed to do here? Why do they even need me?'

She recalls one client who had a tiny little bump that hardly suggested she was seven months pregnant. Her husband was a doctor, and together they lived in a converted warehouse in the East End. 'I walked in, and she was like: "I'm sorry! I'm so appalled that this place is such a mess." I was like: "What are you even talking about? The place is perfect!"'

The woman explained that her regular cleaner, referred to as 'our treasure,' had been off for several weeks with a bad back, and that after muddling by in her absence, she could no longer stand the state of the place. Michele looked around. Everything was dazzlingly clean.

'What could she see that I couldn't? What was I missing?'

Being required to clean a pristine house owned by a woman with impossibly high expectations of hygiene isn't an easy gig. Whatever you do, it will never be enough. Michele much preferred the dirty houses. The tips.

'Oh, the dirty houses were the jobs I loved because anything I did there made such a difference, and the people weren't so bothered because any improvement was *an* improvement. You didn't feel like you were going to make it worse because you had used, say, the wrong cleaning product for a particularly posh architectural surface made of some amazing mineral you've never heard of that can only be used on kitchen work surfaces, you know? Some kind of special cleaning product that costs, like, 50 quid. I didn't like the perfect houses, the kind where you couldn't use Vim with confidence.'

She soon began to pick up on her clients' peccadilloes. 'Some didn't like streaks in the shower stall. Streaks were the worst. They didn't like soap scum. They would teach me to use those wipers, and wipe in an S shape. It was complicated.' She had to watch instructional videos online at home in order to learn how to do it properly. 'I think that's when I reached my lowest point,' she says, laughing. 'Watching YouTube videos on how best to clean the shower enclosure. I think that was even worse than going to a party and having to confess what I did for a living.'

In time, she grew to not like clients with money. More specifically, those who expected you to take your shoes off at the door. The immaculate residents of power couples who placed a little too much importance on their kitchen islands and wet rooms. She learned to be wary among these people.

'You see their dynamic pretty quickly,' she says. 'You see that the couple are trying to be nice and polite and grateful, but all sorts of things are going on underneath.'

She remembers the home of one particular young couple where the woman stayed at home to look after her toddler, while her bespoke-suited husband went out to work. She was obsessed with dirt. Every surface had to be cleaned in a certain way. Every product had to be ecological. Michele found that the green sprays never worked as well as the hard, cheap stuff from Wilko. The hard stuff killed everything it touched. The ecological equivalents required more elbow grease. The contents of this house needed to be wiped down and repeatedly rinsed because their toddler had a habit of crawling everywhere and licking everything.

'So the woman would just follow me around the house telling me to rinse. After every wipe, rinse. Rinse, rinse. But this just doubled the time on the job. You know, I come from a generation where you put dishes in the sink in soapy water, and don't worry about the suds afterwards. Rinsing was not part of my vocabulary!'

She had to adapt to these hi-falutin modern ways, and the curious folk who liked their dinner plates free of foamy sediment. But she found the attention to detail—all the incessant rinsing—unnecessary and exhausting. 'I said to her one day: "Don't you think that if your baby licks anything he shouldn't, you could just tell him not to lick it again? Like, a life lesson, right?" She just stared at me. Appalled.'

Michele kept rinsing. A few weeks later, the grandmother arrived, which allowed the woman time to go to yoga classes, Pilates, or, in Michele's words, 'some other similarly yummy mummy thing.' The woman's mother was left in charge of the child. 'But the moment she left, the grandmother would go out onto the balcony and just smoke one cigarette after the other, whatever the weather. I loved her! She couldn't smoke in the house, of course, in case the baby came along to lick up all the ash, or something...' Michele, both home help and confidante, kept the pensioner's secret.

She was often called upon to be complicit.

'One time,' she says, 'I cleaned this gigantic house in Stoke Newington over the summer holidays. The mum was taking the kids away for the day, but kept forgetting things and came back: for nappies, sippy cups, whatever; the accoutrements of toddlerhood. The father was staying at home, ostensibly to do DIY, which he told her would be done by the time she got back. Thing is, he had no intention of doing anything of the sort. The moment she left, he switched on the cricket, and sat back to watch it. It was funny, because I could feel the palpable sense of relief that came off him, as if to say: "Fuck! Brilliant! I'm on my own at last!" I knew what his game was because it was a game I used to play myself, so I gave him this conspiratorial look: *I know what you're doing*!'

There were times when clients felt her presence all too keenly, and did not appreciate being quite so observed, and known. At one household she visited on a weekly basis, the wife was ill with a degenerative disease. The couple were compulsive hoarders. Their basement flat was perpetually dark. Damp mouldered in the corners.

'Going into that flat, I didn't even know where to begin. There was just so much rubbish, so many alternative medicines alongside all the normal medicines, a lot of dirt, so much mould, and this awful damp that just hung in the air. It should have been condemned, frankly. It was the most awful place.'

The owners were people who had, in one sense, already given up on life. The man had become his wife's full-time carer, and the strain was beginning to show. Michele wanted to help however she could. One morning, in the second bedroom, she moved the bed away from the wall in the hope of finding rubbish that she could legitimately throw away to bring back a semblance of space and cleanliness. Beneath the bed were plastic bags filled with pornographic magazines. 'I didn't know what to do, whether to pretend I hadn't seen them, or just stick them in a neat little pile? What the fuck was I to do? I just put them back, more tidily than they had been before.'

Her efforts were duly noted. When she went back the following week, the man was palpably embarrassed. He couldn't meet her eye. Eventually, he fashioned a conversation, the most awkward sort of icebreaker. He told her that a lot of the stuff in the house was, 'quite silly, you must ignore it.' He could have been talking about anything, of course, but Michele knew what he was referring to.

'He was trying to let me know that he knew I'd found his stash. I think he felt I was judging him. But I wasn't! You know, clearly, because of his wife's condition, he hadn't been able to have normal sex in a long time. There were pictures of her throughout the house, of their wedding day, and she had been a beautiful woman, absolutely gorgeous. The disease had devastated her. So the whole situation was really sad, and I just thought: You poor sod. I wasn't judging him for having a wank, and it's not like he was seeing another woman. But of course this was a conversation we couldn't have. I wasn't his friend: I was the cleaner.'

Michele was the cleaner, a role whose requirements were clearly delineated. At least in principle. But who cares for principle when there is ironing to be done? Ironing was not always included in her cleaning requirements, not officially.

And yet there was always mountains of it to do.

'So I'd be there, cleaning around the house, getting on with my work, and at one point they would say to me: "Oh, you wouldn't mind just ironing that pile of clothes over there, would you?"' she says. And the cleaner, wanting to please, to keep their job, to earn their money, would accede. But ironing takes time. Michele once lost a job over ironing.

'It was the fourth time I went to this place, I think, and I must have relapsed. I either showed up on the job pissed or hungover, can't remember which. But I did the whole basket of ironing without actually plugging the iron in! Never noticed it!' She roars with laughter. 'The owner called me the next day saying: *I don't think this is really working out, do you?*'

One of the things she did come to enjoy, perhaps more than she might have anticipated, was the relationship that can develop between employee and employer, between client and cleaner. 'Most of them, I found, bend over backwards to accommodate you. They all feel that mild British embarrassment of actually having a cleaner in the first place, and so they work hard to bridge that gap with you. And that's good. It means I never had to work for anyone who was completely awful.'

Very often, people worked hard to establish a rapport with her. She was American. A novelty. Eloquent, too. They liked that, irrespective of the damage done to any supposed hierarchy that would otherwise have existed. There were some clients who would sit her down upon arrival, offer her a cup of coffee, and chat. 'Sometimes the conversation would revolve mostly around cleaning, which means I had a lot of discussions about limescale problems, but you like to engage with them, I suppose, because you know what they are trying to do: they're trying to be kind, nice. In some cases, I could tell they felt a bit sorry for me. Thing is, I didn't particularly need anyone to feel sorry for me.'

Growing up in New York, Michele's own family, though hardly well off, had a cleaner, and no one had felt sorry for her. Their connection to the cleaner was a proper, solid bond. 'I mean, sure, money was exchanged, but our cleaner was wonderful. My mother was quite a lonely and eccentric character, terribly lonely, in fact, but the relationship we had with our cleaner was wonderful. She knew everything about us.'

When she was very young, Michele's father was killed by a train. 'After that, our cleaner became a pillar of strength to the family. She offered us normality. I adored and cherished her.'

Michele eventually gave up on cleaning, even though it had an upside. 'The physicality of it is very taxing, but the effects are tangible. You see them right away. In my writing career, you would maybe get paid, but maybe not. You'd write something, and wait ages for it to come out. Cleaning work is far more cut and dried. I can't say that I actually liked the work, but it was something I could do until I figured out what to do next. It gave me that time.'

She was lucky, she believes. She never had any particularly bad experiences in the role, nothing to sully the memory of that time in her life. She was never abused, though one particular client—an 80-year-old South African—did suggest they get married. 'He didn't seem particularly sad when I turned him down.'

The job gave her an identity when she was in the process of losing hers. 'I did it to escape the dole, to do an honest job. I would rather clean sick up on the streets of Shoreditch on a Saturday night than be on the dole again. Being on the dole is worse than anything; cleaning is better, much better. And it's down in part to you Brits. You are so self-conscious! That makes it easier for cleaners, trust me.'

She grins. 'Don't change.'

Michele is now a chef in a café—simple vegan fare for Hoxton dwellers on a health kick. She has rebuilt her relationship with her children, now grown, and is on good terms with her former husband. Her life is smoother, more balanced. Her time inside other homes gave it a spring clean.

5. The Trade Unionist

Having a Yuliya or a Michele in our lives might make us baulk at the very idea of housework as a personal obligation—of actually having to clean up after ourselves. If we can pay someone else to do it, let's do that, a crucial life hack to de-stress us in a fraught world. And though single men are still more likely to pay for a cleaner than single women, hired domestic help has become so common among families in London that it is practically standard.

Most transactions are cash-in-hand, and while insurance companies recommend we do background checks on the cleaners entering our homes, many of us simply can't be bothered. Only 38 per cent of Brits will check for references, and just 21 per cent will agree a written contract. The majority of cleaners are left unsupervised while they work. They have earned our trust for the simple reason that most of them are trustworthy. Besides, obtaining references takes time, a shortage of which is often the very reason people seek help.

While older people might express surprise that a family of modest means can afford to employ a cleaner, their grandchildren may consider the expense mandatory, irrespective of budget. University students are increasingly employing domestic help, and many of their accommodation contracts actually require such an arrangement. Landlords are sceptical that students will clean up after themselves, for the simple reason, perhaps, that they were brought up in homes where someone else always did the work.

In previous decades, children were brought up learning how to clean, and the importance of cleanliness, of taking pride in a tidy house. This was a matter of self-respect: nobody wants to live in a pigsty. The phrase 'tidy your room' was less the opportunistic suggestion it is for children today than an absolute rule. Dinner would not be served before order was restored to teenage bedrooms. But then we were precious about our houses because, as Yuliya suggests, we ourselves had toiled over the polishing, the dusting and the scrubbing. Now that others do it for us, we no longer fully appreciate the effort. Hygiene happens, like magic, whilst we are looking elsewhere.

Inevitably, then, our children will never fully learn the benefits of homekeeping as long as there are others to do so on our behalf.

***

It's a Sunday afternoon at the offices of the trade union Unite, in Holborn, central London. From down a carpeted corridor noises emanate: squeals, giggles and laughter, all of it high-pitched to Minnie Mouse proportions. I wander down the corridor and peer through a glass door. Thirty to forty women, the majority of them Filipino, are engaged in some kind of exercise dance— arms out, arms up, legs down, and repeat. Another Filipino woman is instructing them. It is clear that the majority of the dancers are newcomers, because they don't really know what they are doing. While half are throwing up their arms, the others are busy squatting, before self-correcting and standing up at the very moment the rest are starting to go down, and around. All of them are laughing like hyenas, a tense, almost nervous sound that in time gives over to something that sounds instead like pure, uncomplicated joy.

'Exercise class. You can join,' Marissa tells me. I point to my knees and politely decline. Marissa is chief organiser here, the founder of The Voice of Domestic Workers. She is a 48-year-old Filipino who cleans during the week, and arranges these classes at the weekend to allow her fellow cleaners to cut loose and unwind. As well as dance steps, they are taught (and urged to exercise) English, basic IT, and their workplace rights. With the motto: 'We deserve access to social life,' participants are offered evenings out, Christmas parties, and day trips around the country. Many have escaped from cruel bosses and, like

Amirah, slave labour. Through social media, Marissa is trying to teach those rights to every newcomer to London and to tell them that, if they are suffering, they don't have to. There is sanctity here: they are stronger together.

Marissa first arrived in the UK in 2004. She had fled her employers after mental and physical abuse. She'd been brought over from Hong Kong, where she had been working for a family for several years. When her boss was transferred to the UK, she was expected to follow. Though reluctant, the promise of £700 per month was tempting to a single mother with three children back at home in the Philippines. She knew that the money would transform their lives.

When she arrived in the capital, the situation was less rosy. She would have to pay for her accommodation, even though she was live-in, and also pay tax. This would leave her just £350 a week. She would have been better off staying in Hong Kong. Too late, she was here now, and for a while she made do. But her working conditions became increasingly strained, and she felt increasingly unhappy. So she did what many foreign domestic cleaners ultimately feel forced to do: she ran away. Finding herself suddenly homeless in a city where she could barely speak the language was a rude awakening.

It was also an education.

Marissa was used to abuse, of all kinds. During one posting, in Singapore, she had been employed by a German to tend to his apartment. He was keen on reflexology, and one morning asked whether she might massage him. He had just taken delivery of a new book on the subject, and was eager to road-test it. Body massage was not part of Marissa's job description. 'Not part of my terms and conditions,' she says. 'But when you are in a foreign country, far from home, it is difficult to say no.' She thought of her children back home. 'So, you know, you have to put up with this sort of abuse.'

She leafed through the reflexology book, and saw that it focused on the feet. Though she had little desire to become quite so intimate with her employer's extremities, she reasoned that it could be worse. At least this way, he wouldn't be naked. She washed her hands in preparation, and took a deep breath.

When she walked into the next room, she found him lying down on his back in bed, on top of the sheets, the rest of his body as unclothed as his feet. From the upright evidence before her, he was emphatically pleased to see her. Her employer had done what many employers that Marissa had heard about seemed so often, and so carelessly, to do: conflated porn with real-life.

'Things like this,' she tells me, 'they happen all the time, but behind closed doors. So no one knows what is happening unless we talk about it. Only that way will people know. Otherwise, it remains a secret. I was treated as a sex object, not a worker. But I was a worker! And I knew I had to get out of that situation.'

What should she do? Her employer, perhaps catching sight of her horror, turned over onto his front, and offered her his back. Marissa had to think carefully about her next move. 'I decided to give him a massage, but a very hard one,' she says.

She began by karate chopping the soft fatty flesh of his shoulders, then harder still around the kidney area, registering a certain satisfaction as he cried out in pain. She told him that it was good, that she was following the book's instructions. For a few more minutes, he acquiesced. But the more scared Marissa became, the harder she began to karate chop, her fear promoting itself into anger.

Abruptly, her boss turned on her, and told her to get out. She did not need to be asked twice. He was humiliated now, and the passive state of his humiliation would translate into something more forceful soon enough.

'I knew that I needed to get out, not just of the room, but the apartment. This was his private home. No one would hear me scream. I could have jumped out of the window, but we were high up. This was a tall building, a skyscraper. I'd die. There was no way out.'

She ran to the kitchen, grabbed two knives from the cutlery drawer, then fled to her room, pushing her bed up against the door. Stories of domestic employees killing their employers, she says, are not unusual. 'If the situation is life and death, often you are forced. Either you kill him or... Well, what will happen otherwise?'

There came a banging on her door, her employer—now dressed—trying to shoulder it open. This he eventually did, clambering over her bed toward her. A big man, he was now red in the face both from effort and a mounting fury. Marissa stood her ground, knife thrust forward. He raised his hands in apparent supplication. 'Okay, okay,' he told her. 'I am sorry.'

'You are not sorry!' Marissa barked back. He was apologising, she knew, only because she was holding the knife. In a brief moment of clarity, Marissa found herself wondering what his wife would think if she came back to the flat. But his wife was away.

Now, she told him to let her gather her things, and go. She didn't want any trouble.

'I still had the second knife with me, behind my back, tucked into my trousers,' she says. 'I needed to protect myself, you understand?'

Marissa is from a small village outside Manila. She had children young and did any job she could to provide for them. 'There is work in the Philippines, but it just doesn't pay enough,' she says, a familiar refrain of the global diaspora of cleaners. 'It is very painful to watch your children crying of hunger, you know?'

Marissa is short and stocky. She looks powerful and not to be trifled with. She wears her age lightly, though. For someone who has worked so hard, and for so long, under such trying circumstances, she remains full of life, a natural energy source, a firebrand. She was one of thousands, if not hundreds of thousands, of highly educated English-speaking Filipinos who were too skilled, and too undervalued, to remain in her home nation.

'So many of us go overseas. We have to. And the work we find, of course, is domestic cleaning. It is difficult, for us, for many reasons, to find work elsewhere.'

They scatter throughout the Middle East and Asia. 'China has opened its doors to us now as well,' she says. 'Macau. There are a lot of rich people in Macau. So we go.'

When Marissa left Manila, her children were under three. Her partner looked after them. She spent five years in Singapore, then a further five in Hong Kong. She arrived in London with a visa like Amirah's—only permitted to work within a private household. When she escaped from that abusive employer, she was on her own.

Eventually, she found another job, this one in Knightsbridge. 'A very rich area, and so many long cars!'

Marissa had never seen a limousine before. She thought they were hearses, and so every time she saw another one, her gaze travelled behind it, looking out for the funeral cortege. 'I thought to myself: why are so many people in London dying? It's not possible, surely!' She felt a rising panic. 'Will I die here, too? So far from home? But I'm not ready to die!'

Her employer, more compassionate than his predecessor, told her what they were. This was her first lesson of living in London. It wouldn't be her last.

Her work in Knightsbridge was hard. She began at six o'clock in the morning, and finished at 10 o'clock at night. Having to pay for food and accommodation ate into her salary. 'This wasn't fair, but I was a foreigner, there was not much I could do. I couldn't complain because if I did, I would lose my job, and if I lost my job, I'd be homeless. I did not want to be homeless.'

The Knightsbridge house was huge, with many bedrooms and fine furnishings, luxury she had never experienced before. Her duties included taking the children to school, then preparing breakfast for the adults before commencing the cleaning. The house had to be spotless, gleaming, without a speck of dust. 'The washing, the ironing, the cooking.' She had to go to the shops every day; the fridge needed regular replenishment. The lady of the house could have done this, she points out. 'But she didn't.'

The work was tiring, but the conditions comparatively fair. She stayed for 10 years. Ten years, she says, of cooking, and shopping, and ironing—'so much ironing, you cannot even believe. They had so many clothes!' Gardening was not within her remit, but the garden seemed unaccountably verdant and required constant monitoring. She took it upon herself to tend it one day, and her employers were so impressed they asked her to do it again. She wanted to ask to be paid extra for this, but could not and it simply became another part of the job.

She couldn't dally in the garden, and had to plant and weed quickly, because she had other household chores to complete before the children came home. Once the children were home, she had to oversee homework. And walk the family dog.

Over the years, the family grew. They had two more children, and left Knightsbridge for Kensington. There was more homework, more ironing. 'My priorities were the children,' Marissa says, 'but of course you need to cook, and you still need to iron, and clean.'

She developed asthma, and found she couldn't keep up. The children were active, bordering on hyperactive. 'I kept saying to my employers that they needed someone else, someone younger, just to keep up with them.'

The husband, a banker, was out all the time, but the wife didn't work. So what did she do all day? 'Sometimes the women in these rich houses, they are the queen of the house, and they are bad. They won't work at all, they won't do anything. Not all of them. Some of them are good, but others not. And it is much more difficult if they are around. They like to socialise a lot. They are very good socialites.'

So the Kensington house was often full, and Marissa had to tend to the guests, too. A lot of tea, plenty of cake. 'The crumbs!'

One day, she was asked to look after the household of a fellow domestic cleaner, who was off sick. The lady here was, in Marissa's opinion, 'a queen.' When she arrived, one of the first things the woman asked her was to locate her daughter's lunchbox. It had gone missing.

'I had to explain to her that I didn't know where the lunchbox was. I didn't even know the child because I hadn't met the child yet! I told her that I had to take her son to school, he would be late otherwise. And then I thought to myself: this is crazy. So I said to the woman: "Look, you take your child to school, because a child needs its mother. I can see that you are not working, so you can do it!"'

Marissa had crossed a line. The woman appraised her coolly. 'I don't think she liked me saying that her son needed her, that children need their mothers. I had to explain to her that if I took him to school, he would cry non-stop, because I was a stranger to him, not the usual person. I had to remind her that she was the mother, and that she should be able to take her own child to school.'

She shakes her head, and lets out a sigh at the things she sees. 'Some of the women are just a little bit too dependent on us, you know?'

After she scolded this mother for not being more present in her child's life, she thought of her own three children, thousands of miles away, about how desperate she was to see them, to be able to take them to school in the morning and pick them up again afterwards.

What if, she began to wonder, there were an organisation to help domestic workers like her and her fellow immigrant cleaners? There was historical precedence here. In the first decades of the 20th Century, one Kathlyn Oliver, a cleaner herself, became increasingly vocal about the rights of servants. There was much talk then about women's rights outside of the house, but what of women's rights *inside* the house? 'Why should the domestic worker be the only one of all the nation's workers whose work is never done?' Oliver asked. Her efforts led to the formation of the Domestic Workers' Union, which campaigned for shorter working hours, better living conditions, and fairer pay.

In the 1970s, May Hobbs, a cleaner from Hackney, campaigned for better wages and conditions in what came to be known as the Night Cleaners' Campaign. Hobbs complained that they were expected to clean up far too much in far too little time and were poorly paid. She organised strikes, and became blacklisted as a union organiser. But she was not easily thwarted.

'From that moment,' Hobbs later wrote in her 1973 book, *Born To Struggle*, 'going round and organising the cleaners became a full-time job for me, especially the night cleaners, who to my mind were the worst exploited.'

She took her demands to the Ministry of Defence, and found support in civil service unions and among feminists. More strikes and 24-hour pickets followed. GPO engineers came out in support, likewise milkmen, postmen, dustmen. In August 1972, her demands were met.

Marissa realised that more of her peers had also been treated badly. Many, too, were poorly paid, overstretched, exhausted, ignorant of their rights. Nobody gets into cleaning thinking it will be an easy job, she says, 'but if you are being treated okay, then fair enough, the job is what it is. Problem is, too many of them aren't.'

In the Philippines, such grassroots organisations might be difficult to arrange, much less engage and motivate others, but in London, she felt, other loud voices would join her own. And London had become her home, having brought her children over in 2009. Their father wasn't happy about it, a subject about which she will only say: 'It is better to have a husband that is dead, because that way there are no questions. But if your husband is still alive, even if he is not present in his own children's lives every day, then this is a big problem. I had to fight a lot.'

The few occasions she does manage to return home, she feels strange. 'London is where I live now, it's who I am. Besides, when I do visit the Philippines, I need a visa. Too complicated!'

She and her family live in the suburbs, each of her children managing a local pizza delivery outlet. Their flat is small, but they have everything they need. I ask whether their house is a clean one?

She looks at me coolly. 'Of course,' she says.

Marissa spends most Sundays at Unite, running The Voice of Domestic Workers. Galvanised by her own bad experiences, and keen to help those forced to defend themselves against sometimes cruel, occasionally psychotic, employers, members arrive here largely through word-of-mouth or occasional Facebook posts.

Marissa runs a website, but often doesn't have time to update it. The vast majority of women laughing like hyenas in the union office— and they are all women—are, like her, Filipinos. They are loud and chatty, and funny, dressed in puffa jackets and artfully distressed denim. Many wear heel-boosted trainers to give them a couple more inches in height: otherwise, they are the size of children. On the day I attend, there are two Indonesian women, one lady from Uganda and one from Nigeria. No eastern Europeans, today.

After the dance exercise class, they convene in the room next door, where they talk about their week, about the issues they are facing, the hostels many of them live in. Between them, they clean in every area of the capital. This is the only time they get to catch up with one another. Marissa underlines the importance of maintaining their own individual Facebook and WhatsApp groups, encouraging them to stick together and to offer one another mutual support. At the front of the room, she stands before a whiteboard and talks about the need for every single one of them to fight for their rights. For people power.

'You have rights!' she reminds them all. 'Nobody is allowed to take advantage of you. The only way you will have access to your rights is if you continue to fight for them. Never forget,' she says, 'that you have a voice, and that we are listening.'

Afterwards, I tell her that what she is doing is invaluable. She nods. Of course it is. 'I am a fighter,' she says. 'I can survive whatever. But not everybody else can, which is why I am here now, fighting for them.'

She says that a lot of the women here have been trafficked, kept against their will. Many have escaped. A significant majority have been abused, both mentally and physically; some have been raped. The idea behind The Voice of Domestic Workers is to bring these disparate individuals together so that everyone is supported by someone. They want what everybody else wants: fair treatment, fair pay, workers' rights. They want a decent standard of living. They want to be acknowledged. Marissa wants us to hear their voices, and encourages them to tell their stories. If we live in a world where the majority are now treated fairly, then what about them, these low-runged, marginalised workers? Why can't we treat our domestic staff fairly, too?

Then she tells me, in her beguilingly brusque manner, to talk to Jennifer. 'Jennifer,' she says, 'is a fighter, too. Go and talk to her. Listen to what she says.'

6. The Lesser-Spotted Male

The first thing that strikes me about Mario when I meet him is as obvious as it is unusual: he's a man. Small but powerful, with arms like Spanish hams, and an instantly pleasant demeanour, Mario invites me into his east London flat with a small but noticeable flourish: ta da. To step over its threshold is to disrupt its perfection, and as I look around, I also look at him. What I see in him is a pride that brims up and collects in his sparkling eyes. The flat is clean, but it is more than that. It's impeccably clean, unerringly so. There is one main room, L shaped, with a double bed in one corner, a guitar in the other, television and sofa opposite. The bed is made so tightly you could bounce coins off it. I am worried about sitting on the sofa because it looks so unsat upon, so very... orderly. On the sole chest of drawers, there are a great many trinkets: small Buddhas, china elephants, myriad African carvings. Everything inhabits its own space, and that space is entirely dust-free.

When I do sit down, I look into the kitchen opposite, and note that it, too, is pristine. I realise, too late, that I didn't offer to take my shoes off when I entered. Perhaps I should have done so? 'It's fine,' he says. I don't entirely believe him.

The next thing he says to me, when we are sat alongside one another, is this: 'Sorry I didn't have time to tidy up more. The place is a mess.'

I look at him and laugh, politely noting the joke.

He isn't joking.

'I had a late one last night, so I've only had time to go around with a cloth. Sorry,' he says, apologising again.

You don't come across many men in this game. People who clean trains can be male, and there are many male office cleaners, and street sweepers. The cleaners that polish the floors of our airports and train stations are often men, but you won't find many pushing a Hoover around somebody else's private residence.

Yuliya had told me that people don't want a man in their house. 'They don't feel safe, or at least comfortable. Only for end-of-tenancy jobs,' she said. 'Otherwise, people prefer women.'

But right now Mario is telling me otherwise. 'Oh, lots of people have told me they would much rather have a man cleaning their house,' he says. 'Perhaps because they want particularly physical things doing: the bed moved, the sofa, bits of furniture. There can be a lot of heavy work. A number of my clients have told me that they have had male cleaners in the past, and I have to be honest with you, that surprised me, because I thought I would be the first one.' He shrugs, palms up. 'But I'm not.'

If many people fall into cleaning by accident or bitter circumstance, then it might be said of Mario that, at the age of 60, he has actually found his ideal job, the role for which he was born. He is qualified for, and capable of, so much more, of course, but Mario, a lifelong Londoner of Maltese descent, takes matters of cleanliness very seriously indeed.

'I might be a little bit OCD,' he says.

Many of us mis-diagnose obsessive compulsive disorder when all we really are is fussy, but Mario is certainly scrupulous about cleanliness. He lives on a quiet, and well-kept, council estate in the East End of London. The financial hub, with its hubristic towers, dominate the skyline, and his block squats below the DLR line. Inside his flat, the few items of furniture—bed, sofa, coffee table—are all white. The huge black TV is currently tuned into a vintage country music channel showing back-to-back videos from Roger Whittaker, the celebrated British folk singer.

When I compliment Mario on the place, he offers more apologies.

'I feel pretty guilty right now, because I was out last night, which is unusual for me, and I wasn't back until quite late, after midnight. I had been planning to clean for two, two and a half hours, because I knew you were coming, but I was too tired, and so all I've had time to do this morning is make the bed, and a quick dusting.'

He's being a little disingenuous and I'm confident he knows this. He is well aware that his flat is pristine, and he takes pride in this fact. I think what he's trying to convey to me here is that he can make it even cleaner, and regularly does. I'd employ him in a heartbeat.

'I clean every day,' he says. 'Every time I use the oven, for example, and I use the oven a lot, I let it cool down for a bit afterwards, and then I clean it, top to bottom. I can't bear a build-up of grease. Come, I'll show you.'

He takes me into the kitchen. The surfaces sparkle in the morning sunlight that streams in through the window. There is not a mug out of place, nor a crumb anywhere. The sink bears no droplets of water.

I wonder how the place could be cleaner. 'I haven't polished the floor, and I should have. I haven't wiped around.' Mario looks anxious as he makes this confession, eyes darting around the place in search of fault.

Mario is divorced and has a grown-up daughter. He clocked up 27 years on the London Underground, working in the ticket office, as a station supervisor, then down on the tracks, then doing the banking. When they began shutting down ticket offices, he left. 'I was offered voluntary severance, or the option of staying on to do the night shift. I didn't want to be doing the night shift in my late fifties, so I took the severance pay, and the pension, instead.'

He spent the first 18 months of his unexpectedly early retirement relaxing. As a single man, he lives frugally. 'All I really needed,' he tells me, 'was a little bit of extra pocket money now and then.' He wanted to keep active, both physically and mentally, and shortly after his 60th birthday he thought about getting a part-time job. Domestic cleaning was his only consideration.

'It was obvious, I suppose. Whenever friends come back to my place, they always ask me how come I'm so clean. They always comment on it, on how clean it is. So I suppose I am a little obsessed with cleanliness, yes. And I liked the idea of doing more cleaning, even if it wasn't my own place. Transforming something dirty into something clean—well, it's satisfying.'

This obsession, he believes, comes from his Maltese lineage. There is something in the Mediterranean mindset, more so than the British one, that values cleanliness. Perhaps, he suggests, it's something to do with it being next to godliness. He grew up in London with five siblings in a small house. 'It was always spotless, the washing was always done, the ironing done, the rooms were always tidy, the beds always made. It's a European thing, definitely. Europeans are very house-proud. Our homes are like show homes, and that's what I grew up with, that mindset. I suppose you could say that cleaning was in my DNA.'

He placed an ad online offering his services as a male cleaner. He waited, he suggests, for no more than five minutes before the first message came pinging in on his phone. 'I kid you not. I couldn't believe it. Within five minutes of putting up the advert, I had a message. Then the phone started ringing, and it didn't stop.'

This was all just a few months before we meet, which means that Mario is still new to the job. It's still a novelty. He tries to limit his work so that he makes no more than £100 a week. This is pocket money, not a living wage. 'I only do two or three houses a day, £10 an hour, but if I do offices, it's a little more, £12.50. Today is my day off.'

Except that it isn't. An hour into our conversation, his phone rings. A woman wants him to come and take a look at one of the flats she lets out for Airbnb. I can hear her talking to him. Her accent is strong, sharp, eastern European. She asks him if he can come in later today, and he pauses for less than a second before agreeing. 'Yes, of course. This afternoon?'

I hear her asking for some references, and he confesses he has none. He says that he hasn't been doing this job for very long, but would rather not put pressure on his clients by asking them to write how well he keeps house. 'But,' he says to the woman, 'I can give you my address, and you can come and see my house, where I live, who I am, if you want. I can show you my identity, you can meet me, and get an idea of the kind of person I am, the kind of cleaner. I don't hide.'

Afterwards, he tells me that he says this to many of his new clients. 'They don't know me, and I'm a man coming into their houses. I want them to know it's all above board, that I'm safe, trustworthy. That's why I say they can come to my house, see how I clean up after myself.'

Though he loves to clean, his new job is not without its challenges. 'I'm very fussy,' he points out. Sometimes, new clients, particularly in offices, think he is too fussy. They don't need him to clean and polish every plug until it sparkles, but are happy with a cursory wipedown. He is learning to moderate his inclinations.

He tells me about his first job, a genuine baptism of fire. 'An absolute nightmare, one of the filthiest places I've ever seen.' The house was in Beckton, belonging to Bangladeshis. He reaches for his phone. 'Here, I can show you photos.'

Increasingly, cleaners use their smartphones to record evidence. When I spoke to Yuliya, she too showed me photographic proof of squalor that she couldn't quite bear to delete.

This family, Mario tells me, had multiple members, old and young, quiet and raucous, and everything in between. The pictures he shows me reveal a house as comprehensively dirty as his is clean. I see that he is not exaggerating when he called it an absolute nightmare. The kitchen looks like a kitchen condemned: dirt, dust, fur lining the oven, the fridge door. There are footprints on the floor, and inside the cupboards, human and animal alike. 'Mice,' Mario says. 'Rats. And the whole family, they just sat there while I worked.'

The owner told him he wanted everything cleaned in two hours, but Mario refused. 'Impossible, I told him. I told him it would take as long as it took, but at least five hours, six.' The man shrugged, and let him get on with it: the Hoovering, the removal of multiple rodent droppings, the heavy duty nature of it all. In the kitchen he found: 'This much grease.' He holds two fingers far apart. 'Even inside the fridge freezer there was thick oil, frozen, and grease. Grease in the freezer? How? This takes time to clean. And the cooker? So so so dirty. That took me an hour and a half alone.'

Again, a certain pride creeps into his voice: this much mess overcome, surfaces made new. Throughout his time there he wanted to ask the family why they didn't clean up after themselves. How could they live in such a state? 'But I couldn't, because at the end of the day, they are customers. I didn't want to offend.'

When he did finally complete the job, many hours later, the owner came in to inspect the work. He looked at the cupboards, the fridge, the oven, the work surfaces, the floor. Occasionally, he nodded his head, but the anticipated—perhaps even hoped-for—appreciation never arrived. He spotted a speck of dirt on one of the plug sockets, which earlier had been covered in a kind of fuzz, and pointed it out to Mario, imperious index finger extended. Mario got down on his hands and knees, and wiped it off.

Now, he says to me: 'You expect gratitude, and you get this instead.'

Mario had worked for almost six hours, which is £60. The man haggled. Mario, too tired to argue, accepted the lower offer. When he got home, he had a very long shower.

This left him not particularly well disposed towards Bangladeshis. 'I'm not racist,' he insists, 'but I can't clean for Bangladeshi or Pakistani families any more.' He says he has cleaned several more houses belonging to people from both countries, and each time he experienced similar mess, ill-treatment, and haggling. 'They just don't clean, I don't know why. It isn't worth my while doing it. They are pleasant people, but the job itself—it's just not worth the money.'

Many of the cleaners I spoke with said that in Bangladeshi, Pakistani, and Saudi Arabian cultures, something like a caste system still exists. Cleaners are at the bottom of the professional pecking order. People in these countries are supposedly used to having staff, servants, in some cases 'slaves,' and so common courtesies are not extended because they are not needed. Orders are barked out, and obeyed. Several cleaners I spoke to told me that they would simply avoid working for people from certain backgrounds. (Unsurprisingly, I know of no peer-reviewed research that backs up the idea that some cultures treat cleaners worse than others and it must remain an anecdotal and unverified view.)

Happily, Mario's experiences have generally been good ones. People welcome his presence. There is one particular elderly couple he cleans for who treat him like a long lost son. They also like to have a masculine presence about the house. 'I think they just want a bit of company mostly, and they are lovely people, and I am happy to talk to them, but I never forget that I have a job to do. They like it that their neighbours see a man walking in and out of the house, so perhaps I am protection for them, in some way?'

He is aware of the soap opera potential to the job, that by regularly inserting himself into a home he can become privy to private lives, to bickering and squabbles. But, he says: 'I want none of that, thank you. I'm not here to see arguments between people, between husbands and wives. I don't want to be exposed to their problems. I am here to do a job, and I want to do it peacefully. If I ever walked into a household where there is tension, then I would simply say to these people: "Call me another time, when you are out, when I can do my work quietly." I'm sorry, but I just don't want that stress in my life.'

The most routinely annoying part of his job comes at its conclusion, when he has to turn to the client and offer his outstretched hand. As his Gumtree ad attests, he charges £10 an hour. But even his more regular clients will challenge him on this, week after week, employing faux innocence and cheap opportunism. He will come to the end of another tiring three-hour clean, and they will maintain eye contact as they say to him: 'How much?'

It never fails to disappoint. They want to barter, to knock him down a few pounds. 'But this is my fee, and it's a fair fee, I think. Do I really have to say it again and again?' His question is rhetorical, but demands an answer. And the answer is: yes, he does, because always they barter. Paying less for what you had expected to pay more can, for some, represent the very sweetest feeling, like a last-minute winning goal in a football match in which fans had been anticipating a draw. Sometimes they will offer him £25 instead of £30, and other times they will say that, actually, they can't really afford to pay him at all this week. 'But they tell me this after I've cleaned, not before.'

Often he finds himself accepting whatever they offer. 'What choice do I have?'

I ask him what he has learned these past few months from people by the mess they leave behind them. He is quick to respond.

'I have learned that children today, and the society that they are brought up in, has changed. When I was at school, we were taught the importance of cleaning, and also how to clean, how to cook. Today, all children learn is how to have a wonderful life, and how everything should be really easy for them. Is this reality? It's not my reality. This is frustrating, because houses in the future will always be dirty, and the people that live in them will always expect people to come to clean up after them. They will have forgotten how to do so themselves, or never learned in the first place.'

But Mario quickly shrugs this off. He's no philosopher, no psychologist. He just wants some extra pocket money, and things to do during his otherwise empty days. Cleaning has given him a new purpose, and every day he is working in what is his specialist subject.

He wants now to talk to me about cleaning products. 'To tell you the truth, cleaning products are just scams, most of them. I'll tell you what the best cleaning product is, shall I? Water. All these chemicals are just included in these products to make money, but all anybody really needs is water, white vinegar and a cloth to wipe everything down. You can't beat it. All these people are getting things like Cillit Bang. I mean, okay, that does help to remove grease, it's a greaser. But then so too is vinegar. I would say you don't really need chemicals. Bicarbonate of soda is good, too. That's what I use to clean my kitchen, and how does it look to you?'

I tell him what he wants to hear: that it looks clean. He responds with a great beaming smile.

7. The Cleaner Who Returned Home

Sometimes, cleaners go back home, to pick up the pieces of the life they had left behind. They find that they've had enough of it in London. They have felt too unwelcome for too long, in a lifestyle far from comfortable. They are ground down by the endless hard work, the miserable digs, the homesickness, the poor long-term prospects. They come to decide, deep down, that they are in agreement with the muttering mantra of the odd passing racist: that they should go back home. Perhaps that would be best—to return to where they came from, to where they still belong, among their own people, far from here.

Zofia came to London from Poland in 2010. She had heard from a friend that there were ample work opportunities in the UK, more she would ever find in her home town of Wrocław. She had nothing to lose. Her friend had recommended Leicester, as she had worked there herself the previous year. All Zofia knew of Leicester was that it wasn't London, that it was further north, but not too far. 'Not Scotland,' she says with what may, or may not, be relief.

Leicester it was, then.

She arrived in early summer with a clutch of numbers stored in her phone: fellow Poles who might put her up for a few days, a week perhaps, and steer her in the direction of casual work. There was a small community of expat Poles in Leicester, and she was welcomed, sort of, but also seen for what she baldly was: competition to everybody else already there.

'Everybody, they want the same job,' she explains.

She advertised locally, in shop windows, and soon began cleaning houses, local B&Bs. She cleaned offices, shops. Sometimes, she picked fruit for supermarket chains. Other times she sorted good apples from bad on conveyor belts. Her days swallowed up hours, and she saw precious little of Leicester. What she saw was enough.

'I was in England, which was good. I always want to see England. But it was London where I wanted to be.' She wanted to see for herself if it was like the films and TV programmes she had grown up watching. 'I wanted to see Piccadilly Circus, Trafalgar Square.'

She saved her money and didn't send any home. Zofia was young when she arrived, 22, and single. Her parents were in employment back home in Wrocław, and though they could have used some extra money, they were not dependent on her. She could be free, and think only of herself, at least for a time. So she saved up, secreting her cash-in-hand proceeds under the mattress, mistrustful of foreign banks so soon after the global recession. Once she had accrued enough for a one-way bus ticket south, and sufficient funds to put a roof over her head, she left.

She knew no one in London. She spent her first couple of nights in the YMCA off Tottenham Court Road, then found a hostel near Archway. She had already been advertising her services online, and had secured cleaning work in Kentish Town, Brixton and Kennington. 'The tube,' she says. 'I couldn't work it out. So many lines!' A potential client in Covent Garden got in touch to say he was interested and she had heard of Covent Garden. 'The opera, yes?'

She moved to Ealing, where there is a big Polish community, and started cleaning in Acton, Brentford and Shepherd's Bush. Hounslow, Hatton Cross. She found a room in a house in W13, and spent one bewildering Sunday negotiating IKEA in Croydon, unaware there was a closer branch in Wembley. 'I liked the meatballs,' she notes as an aside. There were nine people in her houseshare, most of them Poles, and a couple of Lithuanians who kept to themselves. Much inter-house activity revolved around the microwave and the kettle. The bathroom was a nightmare.

'Form an orderly queue,' was the repeated joke of those most conversant in English idioms.

Zofia had rudimentary English, and had planned to attend classes until she realised how much those classes cost. 'So I teach myself, from the TV,' she says. 'Love Island, Big Brother. The BBC.'

Presumably speaking with British people helped her, too? 'Yes, but I don't meet any British people,' she says. 'Not to have conversations with.'

Those she spoke regularly to, who became friends, were from back home, or near enough, and so she remained mostly monolingual. Several months into her stay, and she realised that the only English words she could say with confidence were 'please' and 'thank you' and 'where is the Hoover?' She could say 'coffee,' 'two sugars' and 'I see you next week.' It was sufficient.

Over time, in a way, Ealing became a home from home. She got a pot plant for the windowsill, dyed her brown hair blonde, and bought clothes from H&M. She shopped at the local Polish deli, and became ever more intimate with the contestants on Big Brother, so often did she search for updates on house activities online. She came, too, to understand the tube system.

And then she had a romance. She met a man, Kacper, Polish, from Kraków. An electrician who fixed street lighting. Not quite love at first sight, but not far off it. The passion was all-consuming.

Relaxed by leisure and money, a relationship on home soil often takes time to unfold. Online profiles must be considered, then cautious phone calls and texts exchanged. Then there are dates to bars, to the cinema, to open spaces if the sun is shining. You may discuss the new partner at length with friends, and perhaps see them just once a week to start with, so as not to appear too keen. Too impatient. Perhaps you see other people concurrently, because why not? Ultimately, you wait, you pace yourself, and you make them wait, too. There's no rush.

In foreign countries, Zofia suggests, new relationships tend to be conducted quickly, fuelled by necessity, a need for connection, and to avoid loneliness. You can't really afford bars and the cinema anyway, and you don't really know the parks—which are the ones safe to visit, and those in which you might get lost or mugged. She says she fell in love with Kacper swiftly, 'a matter of days.' Their relationship was convenient for them both, gave them a focus out of work, something to look forward to, get excited by, and provide a certain familiarity of home. They went to Polish-friendly pubs and spoke of Poland a lot, with the fondness typical of ex-patriots. Nostalgia for the place you no longer live in is a drug.

She was busy every day by now, too, always plenty of houses to clean for those willing. 'And I am always willing.'

She moved in with Kacper, into another room in another house, this one near Park Royal on the Piccadilly line. Kacper was also busy. He worked days, and then he worked nights, intent, Zofia says, to save up a deposit so that they could get a place for themselves. Working on the roads, he wore a high vis jacket and made good money. He did not drink away the money like he might have in Kraków, but rather saved it, not under the mattress like Zofia but in a proper bank with a proper account number, and a decent interest rate. 'He was very committed to us.'

He bought a car, an old Volvo estate. Did they explore London together, I ask her? Did they spend weekends driving out into the countryside for leisurely country lunches? Did they visit the seaside, Brighton, Hastings, the weird wilderness of Dungeness? In other words, I say, did they get to know their adopted country, and make it their own?

As I ask these questions, she frowns. 'No,' she says. Her expression suggests bemusement, as if to say: Why would we do that? Instead, they went to IKEA together and to a nearby pub. They ordered takeaways. They watched more Love Island, fascinated by just how brazen the British were. They made friends with fellow eastern Europeans, and ate Indian food with them, or Chinese, but always locally. Why bother with Chinatown in Soho when there was a perfectly good takeaway up the road from the tube station?

Zofia liked her job well enough, though it was long and tiring. She smelled of cleaning products all the time, and took many showers. Every few weeks, Kacper would buy her new rubber gloves, a small gesture to show her how much he cared. She liked the people she cleaned for, mostly, though she remained shy in their presence. Zofia speaks perfectly competent English now, but does so with embarrassment. 'I wish I could speak properly,' she laments. 'I wish I took those lessons.'

But her life remained in a Polish bubble, and she didn't really need much more English than she had. Love Island, after all, works almost as well half-understood as it does when you comprehend everything that's being said. You don't need to be fully conversant to appreciate all those bronzed British bodies.

Zofia and Kacper got married. They returned to Poland for the ceremony, to be with their families, their relatives. It was a small but beautiful affair.

The honeymoon, at the resort of Slowinski Sand Dunes, was memorable for the wrong reasons. 'A client texted me. She texted to say that I was fired, that she hadn't been happy with my work for a long time, and didn't want me any more.'

As she recounts this story, urgent red dots flush her cheeks, pinpricks that spread out as they heat up. Tears reach her eyes. 'She knew I was getting married, and then on my honeymoon, but she chose this time anyway to tell me, to fire me.'

Zofia didn't feel anger so much as embarrassment. Though she hadn't ever wanted to be a cleaner, she nevertheless wanted to be considered good at her job. To be fired so cursorily—to be carelessly dispensed with by text because that's how much she mattered—was humbling and hurtful.

'I cried and I cried. I felt so ashamed. Not just because this woman didn't like my work, but that she chose to tell me on my honeymoon.'

Zofia would never feel fully at home in London. She liked her small corner of it, its cosmopolitan throb, the sense she got that, just by living here, she was somehow at the epicentre of the world. There were no comparable feelings back home. She liked the bustle, the smells, the noise, the fact that you could step outside your front door and always find something to do, somewhere to go, even if you didn't venture very far.

But she didn't belong. Life here felt suspended, temporary, even as her months stretched into years, and she moved from single girl to married woman. She found that she missed Wrocław, but also didn't. There was so much wrong at home; she wouldn't have fled in the first place if there hadn't been. But absence makes the heart ache, and she longed to return to a more familiar climate. She was doing okay here in London, and so her confidence swelled accordingly. Perhaps she'd be able to do well back at home, too?

Also, she wanted children. She wanted them to be Polish, not British. This was important to her.

Kacper was keener to stay. He liked it in the UK, and he liked his work, and the fact that it paid well. Being paid well was a balm in all sorts of ways. They sold the Volvo, and got a second-hand BMW that ran like new. They had their own rented flat now, small but perfectly formed, in East Molesey, always kept clean. He continued to put in the hours, often sleeping during the day while

Zofia was out cleaning, meaning that she would return in time to make him his packed lunch, and then kiss him goodbye as he went off to make road lights work along dark and deserted stretches of motorway. Alone, Zofia would watch more British television, ITV, Channels 4 and 5, fun froth that didn't require her brain to engage. She was, after all, exhausted. She wanted to switch off.

'Work, watch TV, sleep,' she says. 'Life.'

When she became pregnant, Zofia suddenly had that firmer purpose she had been seeking. She was 27 years old, and naturally brunette again. She and Kacper began in earnest to house hunt. They wanted to own somewhere—bricks and mortar the best way to establish themselves in the country, Kacper still insistent that the UK was ultimately better for them. They should stay and make something of themselves. When they did eventually return to Poland—a proper family, comparatively wealthy—they would have earned the respect of their parents, friends and neighbours.

But securing a mortgage proved difficult. They had too little deposit, and were not offered anywhere near enough, not if they wanted to remain in the city. 'The houses here,' Zofia says. 'So expensive.' They would settle on a neighbourhood, in Zone 3, and then 4, and then 5, and then 6, and found that they couldn't afford anything adequate for a growing family.

'It was frustrating.'

They were still looking when their first child, a son, was born. 'Perhaps we should think again of returning home?' Zofia would tell Kacper, gently but now more firmly insistent. She didn't want UK citizenship, didn't want to belong here any more than she already did. In truth, she also didn't want to remain a cleaner, and couldn't see any other viable profession available to her if they did stay.

'I had studied photography at college,' she says. 'I used to take pictures.'

The next few years proved an entirely typical whirlwind for a young family: work, parenthood, house-hunting. And, for Zofia, a pining that wouldn't go away. She was dislocated. Only one thing, she became convinced, would reconnect her to herself.

Returning home.

***

Zofia and Kacper left London, and the UK, and went back. They have two boys now and live in a town not far from Wrocław. Kacper still works as an electrician. The pay is lower, with little overtime, but the cost of living is a fraction of what it is in London and so, Zofia insists, 'it all works out in the end.'

In the years she's been back, she says that she has forgotten a lot of her English. Whenever she is required to speak it, as she is to me now, she does so via Kacper, who translates. More often, she writes out her answers on WhatsApp, letting Google translate.

She admits that the problems that had made Poland so difficult to live in have not entirely gone away, but there is a satisfaction to being home that makes up for that. 'Everywhere has its problems—the UK as well, right?'

She no longer cleans houses. Instead, she has returned to photography. There is not yet much work, but her research has shown that family portraits are perennially popular in Poland, most households giving over at least one living room wall to professionally composed images of growing families. Zofia is setting herself up as a portraitist, and practises on her own family, her two boys. She sends me glossy photographs of her children at play and at rest. She knows how to frame a photograph. Her pictures compel.

They have bought a plot for a house, which is being built to their specifications. Zofia sends me a computer-generated image of what it will look like when it is complete, a handsome, two-storey building set within its own grounds, lots of green space, trees in front and behind. A paradise in miniature. The floor plan shows a lot of space: three bedrooms and a large living room and kitchen. A garage. She sends me a photograph of the plot itself, showing an enormous lorry depositing materials for building.

Zofia and Kacper would never have been able to embark upon such a grand design had they stayed in London, but then precious few would.

'Hopefully the house will be built within two years,' she says. 'It's exciting.'

Not every one of those who arrives in London with big dreams manages to escape, and fewer still seem prepared to return back home at all. But Zofia has. The big dreams that failed to take root in the foreign city are now materialising on home soil.

I text her and ask if she is happy, if she misses London, or if she is glad to be back home.

'Am I happy to be back? I do not know!' she writes.

'I am happy because we were able to buy a beautiful plot [for our home], and I'm happy that my husband has a job that he likes, and I'm happy because I came back with children who are less sick here and can speak in their native language at school, and they no longer ask why we can't live close to the family.

'But I sometimes (even often) regret that we came back—usually when I can't find a job or my neighbours annoy me ;-). We are currently renting a flat but I think that in two years everything will change. We will have our home, I plan to do a photo studio there. I am currently looking for internship in a bank.'

But, she admits: 'I don't have a lot of chances to start my internship because [what counts here] are friends, not a diploma.'

What she means is: it's not what you know, it's who you know. And she doesn't know the right people.

'I would like to be able to find a job by myself,' she says.

Nevertheless, she is home, sustained by a sense of belonging, a sense she was never able to fully achieve in London.

And that, she concedes, will have to do.

A day later, she writes again.

'Many Polish people [have] very terrible flaws: jealousy, envy and interruption in the lives of others, and I guess that's why I miss England sometimes. I know that after 2 years memories look differently. Most of you I will always remember with a smile on my face and a tear in my eyes. And to all of you, people I have worked for, I will always be grateful, one for help, goodness and kindness, others for life lessons. I always remember every kids happily... my wonderful helpers.'

8. The Crime Scene Cleaners

Mopping up at crime scenes and some other unusual places has considerably boosted Maxine and Jasmine's fund of stories. There was the time, for example, they went into a bedroom with the intention of cleaning it, and came across a pint bottle filled with human blood. Another bedroom, on another day, when the mattress was strewn with the detritus of drug paraphernalia and so very many stains, not all of which were immediately identifiable. They've dealt with composting food of such an advanced state that it was already on its way to becoming something else entirely, and forgotten items of clothing that had rotted away long after the moths had left them for dead.

Oh, Maxine adds with a light-hearted smile, there was also that other time when a man, a schizophrenic, took so unkindly to Jasmine's presence in his flat that he picked up a knife and threatened to stab her with it.

Jasmine is eating while Maxine, her mother, is relaying this particular story, but now she puts her lamb kofte back onto her plate, wipes her hands on her napkin, and takes over. Her eyes grow wide as she conveys the horror she felt at the time.

'He didn't like people in his house, didn't like them cleaning up his things,' she relays. 'When he realised that Mum wasn't going to be here with me on this particular day, that it was just me and one other member of staff, he took his opportunity. He was clever, you know? He knew what he was doing, how to manipulate the situation. He said to me: "What would happen if I asked you to leave?" I explained to him how important it was that he had a clean house to live in, and that I was almost done anyway, just another half hour or so. He then asked me if I actually needed to be in the house while I cleaned it, and I told him that, yes, I did. Obviously. Look, I said, the place would be a hazard otherwise, not safe to live in. He didn't want that, I asked. Did he?'

He was an older man, perhaps in his early sixties, and Jasmine thought she had the measure of him. But he was imposing all the same. The look in his eyes was not friendly.

It was at this point that the man went into the kitchen, opened the cutlery drawer, and pulled out a knife. It was a big knife, the kind that would make short work of a watermelon—or Jasmine's torso. No longer calm, he approached her at speed, waving it, shouting loudly, telling her that he would stab her.

Jasmine assessed the situation. She looked from him to the front door, and back again.

'I left,' she says. 'I ran.'

She picks up her lamb kofte, and resumes eating. Beside her, still smiling, Maxine adds: 'Our field of work, it requires a lot of risk assessment, you know?'

Maxine has run her own cleaning company in Luton for the past 13 years. She and her staff used to clean colleges, then hospitals. The hospitals then employed her to clean the residences of some of their patients who suffer from an array of mental health conditions, schizophrenia among them. Maxine is well-placed to do such work. She has a degree in psychology and counselling. In purely theoretical terms, if a knife wielder is among her many clients, she should be able to deal with him.

'He was all right with me cleaning his place, but he didn't like it when I wasn't around to accompany Jasmine, that's all,' she says. The pair of them went back the following week, Jasmine stepping back into the lion's den like a young doe. 'But he was fine this time, good as gold.'

Maxine and Jasmine, who live in Luton, do all sorts of cleaning work together. They have recently begun to specialise in crime scene clean-ups, entering premises shortly after Luton's Crime Scene Investigation team have removed their police tape, bindle paper, electrostatic dust lifters and glass vials, their forceps and, in some instances, the murder weapons. Crime scene investigations tend to be even worse than deep clean commissions, and deep clean commissions are bad enough. Where their work is concerned, pint bottles filled with human blood are not entirely uncommon.

It can be disturbing. Not so much for Maxine any more, she's seen it all, but her staff haven't. 'It's true, they can be quite distressed by some of the places we visit, and some do quit as a result, telling me they just can't do it any more, can't take it. Take yesterday, for example. Yesterday, we cleaned this apartment where there was blood everywhere, the floors, the walls.'

Another murder? 'No, just this man with mental health issues. He scratches his legs all the time, but hard, you know? Often, he hits an artery, probably because that's what he was aiming for. Hence all the blood. You step into a house and see that kind of thing, and it stays with you. It can upset you.'

Maxine, who is 53, has a long history of psychiatric and youth work. She has specialised in working with people with mental health issues, and so cleaning up the houses of such individuals is merely an extension of her job. It's her calling.

'It's what we do,' she says, with a matter-of-fact pride. She picks up a morsel of food from her plate—we're in a restaurant in Edgware, it's after eight, dinner time—and pops it in her mouth.

Years previously, Maxine was working with the Luton Law Centre, helping them with their case books, with eviction notices, and dealing with some of the more vulnerable members of society. She wrote letters, helped caseworkers, and felt a powerful sense of connection to the job. She was fascinated by the machinations of law, at once so complicated but also such a lubricant—intrigued by how it could make happen the things that needed to happen in pursuit of positive outcome.

'I thought: I like this, I should study it.'

But further investigations revealed just how much it would cost her. Back then, she had two young daughters to provide for, and neither the finances, nor the time, to pursue her interest. 'So that was the end of me and law,' she says, shrugging.

But Maxine is not one to dwell on missed opportunities for the simple reason, she suggests, that life is full of other opportunities. She would simply look elsewhere.

Months later, a friend alerted her to the fact that a local launderette was for sale. Might she want to buy it? She didn't think twice. She took out a loan, and bought the launderette. Later, after selling it, she heard that the local college was putting out a tender for a new cleaning contract. This would be regular work—good money. Maxine didn't own a cleaning company, but how hard could it be? Born and raised in Britain, but of Jamaican extraction, she comes from a large family where cleanliness has always been held in high regard. Extended family members get together most

Sundays for church, after which, Jasmine says, 'we go back to my grandmother's house for lunch, and a big clean-up. The house is always spotless.'

Maxine corralled friends and former work associates, and was suddenly able to boast a staff of 25. Aided by her background in youth work, she won the contract, and promptly found herself in a position she had never even previously considered: the boss of a thriving cleaning company.

All went well for a few years, until the tender came up again. This time, it went elsewhere. 'So I had to look for more work.'

This she found in a local hospital. She invested in professional machinery, industrial vacuum cleaners, hulking floor polishers, and more staff. Her new bosses were impressed. They called her in for a meeting, and offered her a regular sideline: being sent to the houses of both patients and the newly-discharged whose complicated array of health issues often prevented them from looking after their own homes.

Now she had more work than ever, covering Luton and beyond, specifically the northern parts of the Northern line that stretch from London out towards Middlesex. Jasmine, who had been cleaning with her mother on an ad hoc basis since the age of 12, after school and at weekends, and during the summer holidays, came on board.

'I didn't get paid at first, at least not when I was still at school,' Jasmine, who is now 25, says, 'but Mum did pay my phone bill.'

Cleaning for people with mental health issues throws up some challenges. The people she has on her books can be private, shy, possessive. They can be overly protective of all their worldly goods, and impervious to the presence of dust, the buildup of bacteria. They might neglect the washing up, might forget to buy bubble bath, shampoo, soap. Food. They might not take as much care of themselves as they should. Maxine is employed as much to talk to these people, to offer them friendship, as she is to clean up after them. She writes reports that get sent back to the hospital for patient monitoring.

Many of the people she cleans for are lovely and docile, grateful of her company—others are prone to violence.

And then there are those who are simply, in Maxine's words, 'perverted.'

When I ask for examples, it's her daughter that answers. 'Oh, you know. They want me to wear a frilly skirt, or a maid's outfit.' Jasmine has learned the art of diplomatically deflecting such attentions where other people might respond more impulsively.

Maxine explains that the 'perverted' quota are exclusively men, and mostly single men. They have mental health issues that prevent them from going out much. To a certain extent, they have given up, and no longer engage with the wider community. Where once they knew how to conduct themselves around people, they have now grown lax, careless.

'These are the kind of men,' Maxine says, 'who leave their chatline cards all over the sofa, and their ganja on the kitchen table. Couldn't give a monkey's, frankly. They just sit there on their sofas, smoking themselves to death, junkies more often than not, and they try to get their kicks wherever they can.'

If, on the page, Maxine sounds like the kind of woman not to be trifled with, you should meet her in person. Small but muscular, she is propulsively friendly, warm and generous, has a slight, sideways smile, an uproarious laugh and bright, dancing eyes. But it is clear that she brooks no cheek, no backchat. Her guidelines are firm. If she is to clean for you, you will not take advantage of her.

Some try.

She says: 'Let me give you an example. You walk into a house—and we always go as a pair, never alone—and there are three men there, all in the living room, all on the sofa, smoking their weed, barely looking up at us. You know that they are not going to move for us, even when it's time to clean up in that room. That's the point when I will tell them: "Okay, we're not cleaning up the lounge today because there are too many people in here, and it's not fair for my staff to have to step over all your feet." I tell them to leave if they want us to clean; otherwise, we'll leave it until the following week.'

Some of her clients are remiss at even the most basic aspects of cleaning up after themselves. They'll flush the chain, but not make the bed. Activate the microwave, but not empty the bins, so that by the time she arrives, they have overflown, a volcanic eruption of packaging from the many days' previous meals, spreading across the kitchen linoleum like plastic lava. 'You expect me to pick all that up?' she says to them. And then, to me: 'I'm no one's slave, you understand? I get them to pick it up themselves. They've got to learn, and for their own sakes, right?'

Maxine branched out into crime scene cleaning a few years ago, and then into pest control. Gradually, her company is cornering the market in her part of town. 'These are very specialist areas,' she points out. 'And in an industry like this, it's good to specialise, to build up your reputation. Your reputation is everything.'

She says that, in this line of work, you learn much about the human condition. 'It's eye-opening, let me tell you. The things we've seen.'

You also learn a lot about humans in general. In the last dozen years, Maxine feels she has developed a certain measure of a great many people from around the world, as a direct result of having employed them. Many of her staff have been temporary, if only because cleaning tends to attract gig economy seekers. The majority, she admits, have been women.

'Men don't mind this sort of work as long as it involves some heavy lifting, and shifting of furniture,' she says. 'They like to use their muscles, you know? And Jamaican men are happy to clean houses so long as they get to have a full house to do it in. They don't like houses to be empty. Why? Because Jamaicans just love to sweet talk to whoever's listening!' She hoots with laughter.

Over the years, she has employed people from Africa, Asia and Europe. Africans aren't entirely reliable, she suggests, 'though Ghanaians do make for good workers.' But the most unreliable, again in her estimation, are the eastern Europeans, that demographic that has to some extent colonised this industry within the capital.

'Look, if I've had 20 eastern Europeans working for me, then only two or three of them have been any good.' I ask her to tell me why. 'You tell them to go to a house for a couple of hours, and they'll get a couple of their friends to go with them so they can do it in half the time, then get out of there. If you insist they have to stay for the full two hours, you've got problems.'

But why? She shrugs. 'Because they want to be quick, they want to get onto the next job, they want to make as much money as they can.'

When I ask her to tell me about those employees who account for that most rarely cited demographic within the world of cleaning—white and British—she lets out a sigh that sounds like air escaping a tyre.

The only white British cleaners she has ever employed that turned out to be any good, she says, are those with learning disabilities. 'They're good, they stay.' There is a reason for this, it seems. 'It's like with black people in this country 40, 50 years ago. If you're not the brightest kid in the classroom, then at some point you will get told that very few job opportunities exist for you, and so you may as well get a job as a cleaner because there are no other options for you. I'm guessing they said the same for people with learning disabilities, that they have limited options. And so they finish school convinced that they can't do anything but clean.

'It's cruel,' she says, 'but that's the way of the world as I see it.'

And as for those with non-learning disabilities? 'These so-called "normal" English ladies? They turn up for one day, but don't bother to turn up the next. They can't be bothered, and can afford not to, in many cases. Even if they say on their application form that they are single, you know they'll have a plumber boyfriend hidden somewhere... From what I've seen, they'll only sign up with an agency like mine if they can no longer get benefits. Otherwise, like I said, they can't be bothered. It's hard work, you know. The job isn't easy.'

An average shift lasts 13 hours, during which Maxine and Jasmine cover a great many miles, 'in the truck, in the car, often taking our own cleaning equipment from house to house.' Maxine has built up all sorts of opinions on cleaning products. She prefers soap, warm water and, like Mario, a strong arm over branded cleaning products, and sings the praises of one particular vacuum brand—Sebo—with such unparalleled enthusiasm that I find myself googling their models when I get home.

But the work levels are incrementally taking a toll. In her fifties, Maxine is feeling it in her body more. 'It's backbreaking, knee-crunching work,' she says. 'I don't like bending down these days.'

As for Jasmine, she isn't entirely convinced that this is her true calling. More laidback and laconic than her mother, Jasmine tells me that she has found herself a career cleaner because her mother wanted her to work alongside her. She wanted to please Maxine. Which isn't to say she hates the job, because she doesn't. 'It's definitely interesting work, it pays well, and it's a good living.'

The pair have featured on a television documentary about their crime scene work, and as a consequence Jasmine is often recognised in the street as the Woman Off the Telly. 'People want selfies with me,' she beams, incredulously.

Jasmine, who has studied spa management, and health and beauty, at college, thinks she might want to return to education to study psychology. 'Like Mum, I find I've become fascinated by the human condition,' she says. 'I'm focusing on bringing up my little girl at the moment, but after that? Who knows?'

I ask what happens when they get back home to Luton. Do they switch off, can they relax?

Maxine shakes her head. 'Paperwork,' she says. Much of her supposed downtime is spent chasing late payment or missing pay. Many of the hospital references she gets are people with long-term illnesses, some of whom die. She says she has attended two funerals in the last month alone. The bereaved families they have left behind do not automatically think about the cleaners who cleared out their late relative's house, nor the fact that Maxine needs recompensing for the bright yellow skip that sits outside the dearly departed's house, a skip filled to the brim with a tonne's worth of rubbish that Maxine and Jasmine spent several gruelling hours clearing, in order to leave the place empty, and clean, and sellable.

She wishes this part of her job were easier, that she would be paid for her work without having to chase up anyone. But money has a habit of staying in the pockets of others. If she doesn't pursue it, it will never be hers.

When she does get to bed, she likes to listen to the radio, *talkSPORT* and *5 Live*, mostly, brief moments when she is no longer defined by her role, when she can lose herself to discussions on football, rugby, cricket. When she sleeps, she sleeps deeply, and her body goes about its night-time business of reviving itself and giving her the energy necessary to drag herself out of bed the morning after, ready for the endless cycle to resume.

Tell me about your friends, I say to her, your time off and away from work. Is your social circle largely comprised of your peer group, fellow cleaners who get together to let off steam the way, say, footballers, and masons, do?

9. Cleaning for the Super-Rich

Only once during my long research into the work of domestic cleaners am I referred to as 'Sir.' This unearned deference is paid to me by a man who dresses in such a way as to inspire both confidence and respect—an expensive three-piece suit, likely merino wool, with cufflinks that catch the light. He is the sort of person who exists in a rarefied world where all men are 'Sirs,' and all women 'Madams.' Employers of either gender warrant the lofty title 'Principal.'

Vincent Vermeulen, who is refined in attire and speech, is discussing the high net worth individual, a demographic unlikely to be seen on a bus near you any time soon. Most high net worth individuals conduct their business from behind closed, often fortified, doors, and are people from whom the rest of us invariably want something. As a consequence, they are secretive, discreet, suspicious even. Such individuals—those who can buy anything they want at a moment's notice, and whose moodswings can influence the FTSE index—crave one thing over everything else: a simplification of their daily lives wherever possible, oil to grease the cogs that continually turn.

To achieve this, they need help. No rich man or woman is an island, after all. They need tending to. They need people not just to clean their toilets and change their bedsheets, but to assist them in managing every moment of their important day-to-day lives. To ferry them from port to heliport and back again, to provide an overview of each day's impending events and to facilitate their arrival at them in a timely fashion. They require assistance dressing in the morning, and undressing at night.

In short, to achieve something that money alone can't buy—namely, *time*—they need butlers and housemaids. Butlers and housemaids, of course, constitute what we know as 'domestic help,' but at this altitude they are dressed in finer clothes, and come with an education in etiquette and discretion; in other words, people for whom the terms 'Sir' and 'Madam' do not sit like a glass marble in the mouth but rather drip mellifluously from the lips.

In cities like London, the very wealthy don't have to look very far. They are spoiled for choice when it comes to the world's best house staff, individuals who will treat them like kings and queens, and make them feel appropriately VIP.

In 2017, the *Guardian* suggested that London remains a magnet for the global super-rich. It reported that the UK capital continues to attract millionaires and billionaires from Asia and the Middle East, from Russia, and that the number of ultra high net worth individuals—those with assets of more than $30 million—is expected to increase by 30 per cent to 12,310 over the next decade. Estate agents deem London, 'without doubt the dominant city for the wealthy.' There are many reasons why the rich like London so much, but they include relative safety and stable government, lax tax laws, a time zone that conveniently straddles Asia and America, handsome mansions, world-class private education, excellent luxury shopping opportunities, and a professional cadre of accountants, lawyers, bankers, jewellers, tailors, bodyguards—and butlers who cater for their every need.

This is good news for Vermeulen, a Belgian businessman, whose work involves training those that want to become employees for such individuals. He does this in his native Brussels, but also runs offices in Luxembourg and London. Vermeulen comes from a long line of Vermeulens that have worked in service. Though he started out in service himself, he branched out into training when he realised that there was an increasing demand for such staff. Who was better placed to help create the butlers of the 21st Century than someone with his insider knowledge?

In correspondence, Vermeulen is impossibly polite and deferential. I can all but hear him bow obsequiously to me as we exchange emails, and the more he refers to me as 'Sir,' the more

I self-consciously cringe, largely because when I am reading his messages, I am in my office at home, habitually dressed in an old T-shirt and sweatpants.

Face-to-face, however, he is much more genial and approachable, and not at all the haughty stuffed shirt I'd been anticipating. He is middle-aged and jowly, quick to laugh and enormously friendly. But he does nevertheless exude an air of importance, someone to whom a certain deference is due. The dress shirt he is wearing this time is almost certainly silk, the waistcoat cashmere.

He laughs when I tell him about my preconceptions of butlers, and blames *Downton Abbey*. He says that mention of *Downton Abbey* crops up frequently in his line of work. He is grateful for the TV show because it reminds the world of the importance that is placed on the efficient running of a household, but its image of fussy and fusty starched staff is as antiquated as it is outdated.

'Today's butlers and housemaids are no longer quite so subservient, I think you will find,' Vermeulen tells me. 'The "*Downton Abbey* factor," as I like to call it, gives us an advantage because it draws people to the profession, but also a disadvantage because it gives the wrong impression. If we want to understand the role of the modern day butler better, we need more to look towards films like *Kingsman*.'

In *Kingsman*, a 2015 action spy comedy starring Colin Firth, butlers are seen to be more like Q is to James Bond than Carson to Lord Grantham. In essence, they are line managers, but sharp-cheekboned ones, robotically efficient creatures who make their principals' day-to-day lives run as seamlessly as the stitching on their Gieves & Hawkes.

The Q reference, it turns out, is particularly appropriate.

'Technology plays a very strong role,' he says. 'Every butler is in touch with their principal, often every minute if necessary, via WhatsApp. They are tech savvy, like modern day managers, but at the same time they maintain that butler mindset of old.' Technology is all very well, he adds, but there is little point in having a butler if you are not going to also acknowledge the rich history and tradition associated with having one. 'So, yes, they are well dressed, well presented and well spoken. And their presence is absolutely invaluable.'

Also, today's modern butler is no longer necessarily a he, but is just as likely to be a she.

'Oh, we have very many female butlers, and they are wonderful,' Vermeulen says, adding that homosexual male butlers are also much in demand, particularly when working with fashion icons. 'This is because not only do they look good, and take care of their appearance, but many of them really do have a very strong fashion sense, and this is appreciated by certain employers. People in the fashion world like their employees to have a similar eye for detail; that goes a long way. They are masculine and feminine, a little of everything.' Many of the gay butlers he trains at his Brussels base, he suggests, 'are absolutely the best employees I have, and very much in demand.'

Vermeulen's butler training lasts for eight intensive weeks. Candidates are taught how to clean, of course, but also the invisible subtleties of 'how to wait'; how to be subservient with self-confidence; and how to conduct themselves around money and moneyed individuals. This last part, he says, is often the hardest.

'Many people find that they can't cope in an environment of champagne, of million-dollar cars. They get carried away, dazzled. But you know, it's never a good idea to take a photograph of your principal's £100 million Picasso and then post it onto your Instagram page, because your principal won't be thanking you for that. And you have to remember, too, that even if you happen to find yourself driving your principal's Bentley around town, it's still his Bentley, not yours.

'Discretion,' he says, pronouncing the word slowly. 'That's what we teach here: discretion.'

He also trains his staff a trick most stage illusionists would love to perfect: invisibility. 'Oh! This is the most important! Staff have to be invisibly present in the house at all times.' This is where the learned self-confidence comes in—to be permanently invisibly present, says Vincent Vermeulen, so that their employers don't even notice they are there. 'That is the aim here. I always say to my trainees: You have to know what your principal wants before areas have become full: ghettos for the wealthy with no space left to swing a mink. And so the incoming rich have migrated into the outer zones, taking their staff with them. Because building regulations in central London mean that properties must be extended *down* rather than *up* or *out*, London's billionaires have to choose between installing cinema rooms, swimming pools, and bowling alleys in basements in central properties—or seek more space, width, height and daylight in larger places further out. Vincent Vermeulen tells me that they are now very often buying up entire streets in Zones 3 and 4. 'It's surface that they want,' he says. 'So when Knightsbridge gets full up, they go and buy elsewhere.'

Wherever attendant domestic staff settle, theirs is a curious and sometimes bizarre life. Vermeulen tells the story of one particular butler—not one of his graduates—who has lived for 11 years in a grand penthouse owned by his Russian employer. This particular gentleman, like so many billionaires here, has never stepped foot inside his London abode. 'He spends so much time in his various other properties around the globe,' Vermeulen explains. But he keeps his butler on call in case he ever does need to visit. And also because it is less expensive to employ someone to remain in a house in the owner's stead than it is to insure an empty house in the city. Should this particular employer ever decide to drop by, even on a whim, then he will expect that house to have been kept to the same standards as all his other domiciles around the world. His butler can never relax. He has standards to maintain.

He must be ready, and so his phone is always charged. He keeps the many bedrooms fresh with 200-thread count Egyptian cotton daily. He stocks the fridge with fresh milk and eggs and delicacies, and replaces the fruit in the bowls before any can brown or bruise. His days are spent anticipating a knock on the door that has not come so far, but might do one day.

He is alone in his thickly carpeted solitude, taking in the views across London—through spotlessly clean double-glazed windows, again and again. Eleven years is a long time to wait, but this is his job. It's what he gets paid for, and handsomely.

'So this poor chap,' Vermeulen says, 'he never relaxes. He waits. He waits because—well, just in case. You know?'

10. The Naked Cleaner

In the reusable plastic bag that she has brought with her to this south west London chain café, Brandy shows me her recent purchase. 'I've just been to Poundland for this.' She takes out a microfibre duster with an extendable arm that permits easy access to otherwise hard-to-reach corners, where the ceiling meets the wall. The duster is pink and compact now, but can stretch to several feet. 'Perfect,' she says, 'for spiders.' She turns to look directly at me, giving me a loaded stare. 'He's scared of spiders, you see.'

'He' is a particular client of hers, an arachnophobe who sees no difference between a money spider and a tarantula. If it has eight legs, he screams. The whole situation is already somewhat comical, as Brandy explains coolly, because while the man is screaming, he is wearing no clothes. He won't take refuge in the next room, because Brandy is naked as well, and he does like to be around Brandy while she is in the nude. This, after all, is what he is paying a premium for.

Sometimes cleaners go out of their way to be noticed, rather than remain invisible, for the simple reason that it's in their terms and conditions to be just that. They have been booked not primarily because there are slicks in the kitchen and mothballs in the larder, but rather because clients want something... extra. A little dusting, certainly, and perhaps a cursory run through with the Hoover, but more than this they crave human connection, a friendly face about the place—and some titillation.

So while Brandy works diligently away at the cobwebs, her client will be cowering a couple of feet behind her, close but not too close, his panic commingling with a mild sense of arousal, and presumably thoroughly confusing him.

'You've got to laugh,' says Brandy, deadpan.

Ridding rooms of insects is about as technical as Brandy's work gets, for her sort of cleaning is comparatively tame. 'No toilets or blocked sinks, nothing that requires bleach.' Cleaners who clean in the nude sensibly avoid chemicals. You don't want hypochlorite, benzisothiazolinone or butylphenyl splashing onto your bare skin. The average naked cleaner tends to confine themselves mostly to dusting, to ironing, and to making beds with hospital corners. The client knows not to expect much more, but then this is not the overriding reason why they employ a naked cleaner.

The reason is more ambiguous. It's seemingly not about sex, though sex is somewhere in the mix. Brandy insists it is 'nothing pervy.' Some of her clients are naturists. Others are more like voyeurs. Some are married, and permit themselves this single indiscretion knowing that they are not transgressing much, and that what happens here for a couple of hours on an otherwise innocent Tuesday afternoon, in the privacy of their own home, is not enough to warrant divorce proceedings if their wife ever found out. Some are experimenting with their own boundaries and attempting to get comfortable in their own skin. Others are simply exhibitionists.

'I have to tell you that everyone I've cleaned for so far has been nothing but nice and respectful to me,' Brandy says. I ask how many of the men she has cleaned for—and it is only men—have, if not behaved inappropriately, then at least flirted with her, come on to her? 'A few are mildly flirtatious, yes, but they would probably be flirtatious fully clothed, too. But, no, no one has come on to me, not even close.'

Nevertheless, some do react to her nude presence visibly, with increased blood flow.

'Oh, of course they have! But then that's only natural, isn't it? It's an instinctive biological reaction to having a naked woman in the house. But,' she adds, finger raised half mast, 'I've only seen them get semis. No one has ever been, like, ramrod straight in my company. They get a little bit hard, they get embarrassed about it, then flustered, then it goes away, and I get on with the job at hand.'

At the slight, and slightly suggestive, pun, she winks, then laughs uproariously.

Naked cleaning, it seems, is a thing. Just as there is a corner of the internet for every curious peccadillo no matter how unlikely—there is a David Cameron Appreciation Society—so there is a disarmingly buoyant appetite for people who polish bathroom floors dressed only in rubber gloves. According to Laura Smith, who founded the cleaning company Brandy works for, Naturist Cleaners, in 2017, one recent survey found that having a cleaner prepared to take her clothes off is one of the most searched-for male fantasies on Google.

'It's a niche thing, definitely,' Laura concedes, 'but a surprisingly popular one.' She also points out the fact that there are many naturists in the UK—up to four million, says British Naturism—and, 'naturists need clean homes too, right?'

'Laura Smith' isn't her real name, though it is the one she gives me and the one she uses for work. She is originally from a small European country she'd rather not name because, she explains, 'it's very conservative, and I still have my mum there so I don't want anyone there to know about the company I run now.' Suffice to say it's not one of the usual eastern European countries one might automatically think of, not Bulgaria, nor Poland, nor Romania. She adopted the name 'Laura Smith' because it's easier for English people to pronounce than her birth name, which is long and comprises more consonants than vowels. Laura is an attractive 34-year-old who looks a good decade younger, with high cheekbones and pale blue eyes. She came to London in the wake of the 2008 financial crash, craving new opportunities.

'If you think things were pretty bad here in the UK,' she says, 'they were worse in my country. We had to leave. We had no choice.'

She had studied politics back at home, but by 2008 was working as an executive assistant for an entertainment company when her country tumbled into recession. Her husband was doing intelligence work for the army, and was frequently deployed to places like Afghanistan and Iraq.

'We'd just got married, and I didn't like the idea of him facing so much danger,' she says. 'I also didn't like us having so few opportunities left at home. I knew that we had to change our lives, so we came here.'

Her plan may have been an instinctive one, but it was also carefully thought out. There is a steeliness to Laura that suggests she would have made a success of herself wherever she ended up. But when they arrived in London—staying with her sister-in-law in Ealing—she couldn't speak English, which limited her work opportunities. While her husband found security work (he is now in data analysis), she became a cleaner. For someone with her ambitions, this constituted a step in the wrong direction.

'If you are intelligent, then finding yourself in this kind of job—well, it's really heartbreaking,' she says. 'You find that you cannot express yourself properly and this is frustrating.

When you can speak it, language opens doors for you. But not being able to express yourself means that you cannot reveal to people who you really are. And some people feel they can take advantage of you.'

It was not the prospect of low-paying hard physical work that offended her so much as the lack of respect. 'I didn't like being spoken to badly, being spoken down to, you know?' In some of the families she cleaned for, she was summarily condescended to, often in front of the children. 'The children were watching as their mother talked to me like this, and then they looked at me like—well, like I was less than them, somehow.'

She decided to revive her entrepreneurial spirit and resolved to work for herself. She advertised locally as a cleaner for hire, and soon found work. After Ealing, she and her husband moved to near Heathrow, before eventually settling in Epsom, Surrey. If she found that her clients were rude, she would stop cleaning for them. By being her own boss, she could determine her own working environment to some extent. She would not be slighted again.

Surrey proved a warmer climate for her than Heathrow. Her clients were nice, more polite. They were empathetic and prepared to pay a higher hourly rate. She became so busy that she soon began to employ more cleaners, women who also came from her country and with whom she could easily communicate. Business was good. Then she had a baby, and took time off. When she returned to the business, she decided to take things to the next level. Cleaning still felt like a temporary arrangement. It didn't demand enough from her. She wanted more. But what?

One day, she received a call from a local naturist interested in her services.

'He asked if it would be okay that he was naked while I cleaned. I thought about this for a bit and then I said to him that it was fine by me.' Had she cleaned for naked people before, I wonder? Did she have naturist inclinations herself? Her smile is a tight one. 'No.'

The client turned out to be a CEO in his mid-forties, the owner of a well-appointed apartment. He had children who were away at university, and so while home alone liked to remain undressed. This was all new to Laura, of course, a very British novelty, she felt, but she maintained eye contact while they spoke, and found that she liked him. He was no one to fear. 'He was nice, a nice man. Normal. I cleaned for him several times, and we chatted quite a bit.'

He became a regular client, and during one of their chats, over coffee, he suggested that nude cleaning might be a business opportunity for her. He couldn't be the only naturist in the greater Epsom area. Why not target her cleaning business for those who liked to be naked? It could prove profitable, he told her. She could even corner the market.

Now, Laura laughs. 'My head rolled over when he said that. A business idea!'

Google told her that there were already a select few cleaning businesses for clients who liked to be naked, but none specifically for naturists. These other firms offered more deliberately suggestive services, advertising cleaners who would vacuum while wearing sexy lingerie or rubber catsuits, women who were more likely to bring a whip than a feather duster. Laura's idea was to provide naked cleaners, but to keep things above board, for naturists, or people who simply liked to be naked. Yes, clients might well be aroused by their cleaners, but there would be strict guidelines to which they would have to adhere. She didn't want to run a sex business.

She began to advertise, then sat back and waited to see what, if anything, happened next. 'I was surprised, I will tell you, because a huge number of people called me straight away: people who wanted to have their houses cleaned by naked cleaners, and people who were prepared to clean while naked.'

At first she focused on Surrey, quickly cornering the market as her CEO client had predicted, and then moved into central London. Soon, she went nationwide. A week before we meet, somebody in Milan contacted her asking if she might extend her business over there. Another suggested she look into New York.

Perhaps inevitably, she has received much media attention; certain newspapers like little more than soft new stories that include nudity and an opportunity to laugh at it, as if this were somehow a thoroughly British trait. I tell her that the knee-jerk reaction to her company must surely be one of suspicion, that it's all very well targeting purported naturists but how do you police your clients? How do you perform background checks before sending women, who may or may not be vulnerable, into the homes of strangers, quite possibly strange ones? She tells me that they are unable to do background checks, but that they do take their bank details, and request that they read their terms and conditions closely. Lapses in behaviour, she warns, will not be tolerated. She instructs each of her cleaners to call in every half hour during their clean to ensure all is well, and that they are safe.

'I did, like you, think at first that it might all be seedy and unpleasant, but I can tell you that it has all been very professional so far,' she says. No complaints? 'No. None. Actually, yes, just one, from a client who said that the cleaner we sent was too shy, and was hiding behind the sofa! I suppose you can't be shy in this job.'

The more we talk about it, the more insistent Laura becomes that this isn't as titillating as one might think, and the more I come to see what she means. Catsuits would be titillating, she argues, but with the naked form, the more you look at it, the more utilitarian it becomes. It's just another body with its attendant parts. We all have one.

'It's your mind that is sexy. What you project. If my cleaners wore sexy underwear to work, then, yes, they would be trying to be provocative. But when you just have someone walking around in the nude with a vacuum cleaner, then I don't think there is anything particularly sexy about that—especially if you happen to be a naturist, right?'

In the two years that she has been running her company, Laura has received a steady stream of 20 to 30 emails a day from people wanting to work for her. Most of her employees are female—about 98 per cent. Women, it seems, aren't much interested in having a naked male cleaner in their house; so the 2 per cent of men she does employ clean for gay naturists—with, she points out, the same terms and conditions. The same 'look, don't touch' rule.

At £45 an hour, the job pays a full £30 more than the national hourly average. Where most cleaning companies expend a lot of effort managing both employees and clients, things have been running surprisingly smoothly for Laura. 'The clients really are very respectful, and my employees are very happy to work, and to be well paid. You know, many of the women we employ are in their thirties and forties, and they are returning to work after having had children. They want flexible hours, they want good money. And this way, they get it.'

Running the company has taught Laura Smith a lot about the British and their sexual proclivities. 'I receive a lot of... shall we say, interesting queries,' she says, smiling. 'Have you heard of this word before: infantilism?' Her eyebrows raise as she forms the word on her tongue, and tells me that she wasn't aware of it before. Paraphilic infantilism is a sexual fetish in which adults—overwhelmingly men—play at being babies, guzzling from milk bottles and wearing nappies.

'Well,' Laura says, 'I have had lots of people calling up telling me about such fantasies, and asking whether we could provide naked cleaners for them. So yes, people who like being babies, men who want to wear a dress around the house, or perhaps just a skirt.'

To these men, Laura patiently explains the terms and conditions, and stresses what is permitted (look) but what is absolutely not (touch). There is to be no filming on mobile phones, no inappropriate behaviour. They can wear what they want when their cleaners come—babygros, a tutu, pleather chaps—but they have to accept that their cleaners won't be changing their nappies any time soon.

'I suppose I have become more permissive since arriving in London,' she says. Ten years ago in her home country, she wasn't so accepting and didn't quite appreciate just how vivid certain people's fantasies were. 'But London has opened my eyes.'

Not everyone is quite so liberal and accepting, however. As with employees of MI5, she rarely divulges what she does to others. While she has told certain friends, she hasn't told all of them, and also not her parents. Similar can be said of her employees, too—women in midlife, mostly, though the youngest is 25 and the oldest 60. 'They don't always tell all their friends either, it's true, and I can understand that. Not everybody needs to know everything, right? Speaking for myself, I don't particularly want the mothers at the school gate to know what I do for a living. But I really don't see what's wrong with what I do, either.'

Laura hasn't been tempted to become a naturist herself. 'No,' she says. 'I'm fine with my clothes on.' Instead, she has learned to be non-judgemental, to accept people for what they are. If anything, she feels encouraged by those she has met through her work. Many people, within the privacy of their own home, may have slightly unusual fantasies 'but they are polite, they are respectful. They don't seem to be hurting anybody—especially not my employees. They are people who want, you know, a particular service. And we provide it for them.'

***

Brandy, not her real name but rather her Naked Cleaner pseudonym, is a relative newcomer. When we meet, she has been doing naked cleaning for just three months. It's been a busy time. With a mischievous grin, she tells me: 'I'm much in demand!'

If I had difficulty imagining what sort of person might be willing, and brazen enough, to do such a job, then Brandy provides some answers. You need to be garrulous and gregarious, funny and confident. Not shy, not demure. Brandy is all these things. A vivacious 38-year-old, she is articulate and engaging, and has a way of making eye contact that seems to draw you in and make you listen keenly to everything she says. She lives in south-west London with her partner and his two teenage children, one dog and a rabbit. She rides a bicycle, which has a basket for the dog.

Before cleaning, she worked in restaurants, and before that, in pubs. She worked briefly on pleasure cruises that ran up and down the Thames. But for 12 years Brandy, a drama graduate, was a stage manager in the West End and for productions that toured the world. A theatrical stage manager makes everything tick, ensuring that everything happens on time. Brandy excelled in the job by being as loud and impossible to ignore as the A-list actors around her. She certainly has a flamboyance that's difficult to ignore.

'Always been a show off, me,' she says, 'and any excuse to flash my boobs, I'd flash them.' But her outward exhibitionism also served an inner purpose. 'I've never felt particularly comfortable with my body—I'm a bit curvy, you see—so I decided that if I could make people laugh with it, it might change my own feelings about the way I see myself? I was ill as a child, and I went from skinny to butterball. I've never completely lost it.' Making people laugh, she believes, helped her accept herself.

In 2014, Brandy found herself falling out of love with the job. 'You can't do this kind of work if you don't love it any more.' And so she quit, and looked for something else to do with her life. 'But to be honest with you, I'm still looking. Of all the jobs I've done since, I've loved nothing even half as much.'

The stints as a waitress were temporary, until something better came along. And though she shone at the work—she likens working in a pub to working in the theatre for its 'soap opera' nature, and once made £800 in tips in three months—she craved greater fulfilment. This proved hard and soon took a toll. She grew disillusioned and increasingly empty. During our chat the only time she doesn't maintain a steady eye contact is when talking about the depression she slipped into.

Looking down at the palm of her hands, she says: 'Oh, you know, there were some unpleasant relationships, weddings being called off, all sorts of nonsense like that. Basically, I stayed home for a year and didn't go out.'

In time she found some solace, of sorts, in gardening. She had never done any gardening previously. But, she says: 'I think I found I just like being muddy.' She began gardening locally, for neighbours, then extended her reach beyond the neighbourhood. She found a job in a gardening business and is currently training for an RHS Level II, which will teach her the principles of horticulture. But working freelance is difficult. 'I've got the rent to pay, a family to help provide for; I needed a regular income.'

One afternoon, she found herself leafing through a magazine with friends and saw an article on naturist cleaning. Her friends laughed out loud, calling it ridiculous and insisting that they couldn't possibly imagine doing something like that, 'in a million

She began cleaning, surprised by how quickly normal—ordinary, even—it felt. The temperature in the flat was warm. 'I was making beds, ironing.' The night before, she had taken ironing lessons from her mother-in-law, as she rarely irons herself. 'And he complimented me on it, so I must have been doing a good job.'

The two hours went by quickly. 'He was nice, lovely, sympathetic and sweet. And to be honest with you, every client I've had since has also been lovely. Sometimes I find that I laugh the entire time I'm there—and in a good way! We have a nice time, a laugh, a chat. They're always terribly polite, the men. I've not yet cleaned up for anyone who made me feel that I was in a creepy situation, or that they were some kind of perv. If anything, they've gone the other way, and made sure I knew they were gentlemen. They treated me with nothing but respect.'

Nevertheless, a certain awkwardness remains. Some men have been nervous about getting undressed in front of her, others perhaps too eager. There have been clients who, like the arachnophobe, follow her around the house, watching and talking, and there have been others who simply leave her to it, and disappear elsewhere in the house, making Brandy wonder why they booked a naked cleaner in the first place.

Most typically, the male clients follow her around the house like a dutiful dog. They offer to carry the vacuum cleaner for her, to help her make the bed. To dry the dishes she has just washed. 'And, yes, they ogle, of course they do. I'm used to men talking to my breasts when I'm fully dressed, so can you imagine what it's like when I'm naked and they're bouncing around?'

It is almost impossible to talk about nude cleaning without also talking about erections. With a smile, Brandy says: 'It's a biological reaction. If something turns a man on, you do tend to see an instant reaction, don't you? And I suppose I have to say that I find it quite gratifying, really. It means they like what they see. It's a compliment.'

She confesses that she doesn't think she feels particularly turned on herself ('although one or two of my clients are pretty sexy'), but she does feel desired 'and it's nice to feel desired, to feel sexy.'

What surprised her most about undertaking a job of this nature was her very ability to do it in the first place. 'Seriously, I had no idea I could do something like this, no concept I would ever be as comfortable in my skin around strangers as I am now, at the age of 38. It's still such an alien concept, to be naked in a stranger's flat, but when you find that you can do it, it does feel like a massively liberating thing.'

It has given her something she never fully had before: body confidence. The clients of Naturist Cleaners choose the women who come to clean them based on photographs they supply to the company. Brandy says: 'I think the fact that they are choosing people like me, curvy women, real women, says a lot in a culture where we are always celebrating super-slim supermodels. I suppose it means that people like me don't actually have anything to hide after all, and nothing to be ashamed of.'

She has also learned much about men's bodies. 'I can tell you I've seen an awful lot of small penises,' she laughs, adding: 'Not that I'm body shaming, merely saying.'

Her friends are much amused by her latest career move. 'They see it as an adventure, too, and they always want to hear my stories.'

Naked cleaning remains a temporary job, but she has no plans to give it up just yet. The pay is very good and her duties are frequently far less physical than she might have expected. 'One client the other week asked if I fancied doing yoga with him instead. We ended up following a YouTube tutorial for an hour and a half. It was brilliant, though I have to say it did feel pretty surreal looking through my bare legs while doing a downward-facing dog, and seeing a naked man right behind me doing the very same thing...'

Very few people dream of being a cleaner. Rather, it's a job one might do when there are few other options, because of their circumstances, because they have bills to pay. For some it's embarrassing, humiliating even. Many do other things while they clean, to make the most of their time in such a menial occupation. Those who get into naked cleaning do so for other reasons still, and not just financial ones. In an era where we now routinely learn how badly behaved so many men are, it is a relief to hear Brandy talking about her clients being so effortfully kind to her. Faced with the object of their desire so up close, they become boys again. Bashful.

'It's not for me to judge them, I don't think,' she says. 'Perhaps they are doing this because they want to be a bit more adventurous, because they're bored, because they're testing their own boundaries. I'm sure that some of them are married and are not telling their wives about me, but I prefer not to think about that. I just get on with the work.'

I ask her how long she plans to continue doing it, and she tells me: 'I may as well enjoy my body and let others appreciate it, for as long as I can before it gets old and saggy.'

But old and saggy isn't necessarily undesirable. Laura Smith tells me that she still has much demand for cleaners into their fifties and sixties, and for women of all shapes and sizes. 'Many men,' Laura says, 'want real women, not for whatever passes for the ideal.'

'I've had a lot of fun doing this,' Brandy says. 'It got me out of a dark period, and it's been liberating. I've got to tell you, I love it.'

11. Cleaning in Japanese

The Japanese for 'I am English' is 'Watashi wa igirisuhitodesu.' If you need to ask somebody where the toilet is, you say: 'Toire wa dokodesu ka?' To state in Japanese 'I am a cleaner,' it's: 'Watashi wa kurīnādesu.' If you've a pen and paper to hand, and you want to write about your current employment status, it's this: 私はクリーナーです

Natalie is on Chapter Six of her Teach Yourself Japanese course when we meet. There are many more chapters to go, she tells me with an eye roll, and she has already listened to the first six chapters many times over, so complicated and convoluted does it sound to her western ears. 'It's not as easy as French, put it that way,' she says.

But she's keen. On average, she listens to a couple of hours a day, through earphones which hook over her pierced lobes and hold tight while she negotiates a Henry vacuum cleaner, its eyes watchful, through the three floors of the house she cleans.

'It makes the time pass quicker,' she says. 'Also, listening to my Japanese lessons while I'm cleaning doesn't make it feel like such a waste of time. It feels, at least, like I'm progressing towards something, and I can tell myself that the time I spend cleaning the house is at least worthwhile, that I'm working towards something.'

Natalie is 28 years old, and comes from Devon. Eight years ago, she graduated from university, where she had studied art and design. She carries with her a student debt that she hasn't begun thinking about paying off yet. While studying, she made ends meet waitressing. In the holidays, she worked on organic farms around the world, including one four hours outside Beijing and another just south of Tokyo. She particularly liked Japan and wants to return.

The long-term plan, she says, is to set herself up as an artist. She is a printmaker, creating designs by printing them from specially prepared cleats or blocks, making multiple impressions. She talks me through the techniques—relief, intaglio, planographic and stencil. She favours woodcut, a type of relief print, and shows me photographs of some of her more recent work.

It's an ancient art, she says, and, though not a dying one, demand for printmaking isn't huge. She smiles. 'It won't make me rich.'

But it is a passion. And so, as with so many passions, it requires the pursuit of more humdrum work to help fund it. Part of the gig economy, Natalie has had all sorts of jobs. She has done bar work. She's served canapés at Downing Street, at Wembley Stadium, and at music industry parties. She met Little Mix once.

She could get a proper job, but she likes the flexibility of temp work, and the hospitality sector is 'easy, not taxing.' A proper job might bring her a decent wage, and with it that most tantalising of things for someone with student debt: career prospects. But there is nothing that kills off a passion for art than a desk job with endless prospects for overtime.

'This way,' she says, 'I get to work when I want to work. And the work is fine, you get to meet a lot of interesting people.'

But this kind of erratic employment earns too little to live in an expensive city. What Natalie needed was a job with live-in potential. So she decided to advertise herself online as a cleaner seeking accommodation.

'Friends had done similar, not always in London, but it seemed a fairly cushy way of living—if, of course, you didn't mind being a cleaner, that is. I don't mind at all, I've no problem with it.'

Natalie is an atypical cleaner. British, white, middle-class and educated, and dressed in a flower-print dress offset by a pair of Converse high tops, she has lived a comfortable life, a hipster with a nose ring whose backstory does not consist of slave labour, nor the pressing need to feed mouths back home. She has opted for cleaning ultimately because it's an easy gig. It pays.

The grammatical perfection of her online ad elicited swift responses, and soon she was cleaning several houses across London, sofa surfing at friends' houses until she found a position that offered room and board. She was confident that this would come before long.

'You'd be surprised how many places offer room and board,' she says, pointing out that they aren't always rich people, but rather older people, married couples whose children have long since grown up and left home, and find they need help around the house. In many cases, they also crave the company of young people in their lives again.

Natalie now lives in Willesden with her boyfriend, Jack. They occupy a well-appointed attic room—en-suite, decent shower— while below them are the homeowners, whom she refers to discreetly as Mr and Mrs Smith. Mr and Mrs Smith are in their sixties. Mr Smith has early onset dementia 'but he's bright as a button most of the time.' Mr Smith used to be a graphic designer; they spend most of their time together discussing art.

Theirs seems to be a largely convivial relationship, albeit one founded upon certain ground rules. Natalie and Jack don't get paid for cleaning the house, but they do get to live, rent-free, in Zone 3. Breakfast is included, lunch and dinner aren't. 'But the fridge is always full, and they are very sweet, very generous, people. We don't go hungry.'

They are encouraged to be up, and downstairs in the kitchen, to help with breakfast, by eight o'clock on weekday mornings. After that, they are free to work whichever hours suit best— 'within reason, and as long as everything gets done.' Their tasks include cleaning the house three times a week, doing the laundry whenever necessary, and gardening at the weekends. This leaves them a lot of valuable free time, which they use doing part-time paid jobs, Natalie at a nearby café, Jack the local pub.

All four of them will often meet for meals around the dinner table for food that Natalie might have helped prepare. 'It's like we've become a part of their lives, and it's lovely, really.' A bit like their parents, I ask? She smiles. 'Yes, but also not, if you know what I mean.'

When I ask if they are hard task masters, her smile becomes enigmatic. 'I suppose so, yes, and Mrs Smith certainly likes things doing in a particular way.' An example? 'Well, there is a special knife I have to use to clean between the wooden slats of the kitchen table, because it's hard to clean in the gaps otherwise. And all surfaces have to be polished, and dusted, all the cupboards, all the lids, the TVs, the speakers. The windows, the banisters. But that's fine, I understand that.'

Gardening is something they do together, a communal exercise. 'The fresh air is good for Mr Smith,' she says.

The arrangement works well for all concerned. In this way, Natalie and Jack can gradually save up money, a nest egg for more travel in Japan, and perhaps even, in the long term, to put down a deposit on their own flat. 'But probably outside London, because who can afford London these days?'

They are in no rush to move out, and it's easy to see why. 'They are really very laid-back, Mr and Mrs Smith, and we feel like lodgers more than anything else. They sometimes go away at the weekend and encourage us to have friends over, to throw a party—as long as we don't trash the place. They even attended one of our parties once. Our friends loved them.'

The work is hardly stimulating, though. Natalie is unlikely to ever actually enjoy cleaning. Nor will it define her. Hence the Japanese lessons. Natalie can already speak fluent French, and has conversational Italian. When she returns to Japan she wants to be able to get by. She hopes to work again on a farm in a similar set-up to here in Willesden: no pay, free bed and board, and to stay for perhaps as long as a year.

'I could be listening to music while I clean, which would probably make the time pass much quicker, but like I say, a little bit of me feels guilty that I'm not more actively pursuing my career. And so this way, studying while I work, I'm at least doing something for me as well. And that's important.'

Though she isn't yet worried about leaving her twenties behind, she is becoming increasingly aware of time passing. Her parents are, too. They sometimes impress upon her the need to assert herself professionally, and to hurry up about it. Is she really going to make printmaking her life? Doesn't she want to find something more worthwhile to do, something that pays more, has more job security, better prospects? Isn't she keen to settle down, and start a family? And why leave home in the first place—and her mother and father—just to move into another home and a set of surrogate parents? Where's the freedom in that?

For Natalie, she feels that she is simply doing what she needs to do to survive, in her way.

'I'm in no rush, and I've landed on my feet here, to a certain extent,' she says. 'I've really no desire to get started in a career I've got no serious interest in pursuing. I want to pursue my art, I want to go to Japan, and after that I'll see what happens. Patience, you know?'

There's a Japanese saying for that. It runs along the lines of: 'Nintai-ryoku wa sugurete imasuga, sono kajitsu wa amaidesu.'

Patience is bitter, but its fruit is sweet.

12. The Modern Butler

As with anyone employed in the profession of domestic cleaning, there are problems this high up, too. Problems with attitude, with cultural expectations. Wealth was once restricted to people born into money, to those with entrepreneurial instincts, but now wealth is—at least to some—easier to come by. The internet has made fame, even if just the fleeting kind, more feasible for all, and online success is easily monetised. In the world of butlers and housemaids, Old Money is preferable to New. Old has a tradition of living—and dealing—with domestic staff. They are used to having people about the house, to help them dress, and eat, and to run the bath, to prepare for an ambassador's party at the last moment, to arrange delivery of the Ferrero Rocher, and assemble evening wear for a black tie function. There is mutual respect, a long established hierarchy. When I speak to someone who services luxury abodes with waiting staff, including Buckingham Palace, she tells me that, correspondingly, New Money can be difficult to work with.

'New Money people tend to be wrapped up in themselves. They don't yet know how to behave, and so they tend to behave rather garishly—unpleasantly, even.'

Those who amass New Money often do so quickly. 'I know a lot of people who have become billionaires within 18 months,' the same lady—who wishes to remain anonymous—tells me. 'And so suddenly they find themselves in vast living quarters, employing upwards of 15 people. They don't know how to live in this world. It goes to their head. Common courtesy goes out of the window.'

This is why domestic staff entering this world can only do so successfully after intensive training. They are not trained to be spoken down to, and taken advantage of, by monomaniacal oligarchs and YouTube celebrities but rather to be appreciated as valuable components in the maintenance of their day-to-day efficiency levels. When they graduate, they are highly skilled in the business of people management. They are discreet, as Vincent Vermeulen (whom we met earlier) encourages them to be, and absorb some of the elegance that surrounds them, so that when you meet with them, they too seem discerning, and poised, and distinguished.

On occasion, it can be difficult, to the untrained eye, to tell employer from employee.

Upon first introduction to Monika, I deduce, almost instantly, that she is a high net worth individual herself. Originally from Slovakia, she is 35 years old, and radiates the aura of someone used to the finer things in life: airline business lounges, weekends at Val d'Isère, caviar on blinis. She is wearing a leather jacket, black trousers, and sharply pointed boots. She has cheekbones Anna Wintour would appreciate and a pout Bella Hadid might envy, and perfect fingernails and pearly white teeth. She could be a film star or a model. She shakes hands with the confidence of a banker before the crash.

Monika tells me that she arrived in London 14 years ago. Since then she has been a housemaid and, later, house manager, to a number of wealthy individuals. She has been in almost constant work, and it is easy to see why. She came to the capital for the same reason that everybody else in this book did: for better wages and a better standard of living. For more opportunities.

She found them.

'When I first arrived,' she says, in impeccable English, 'all I could really say was: "Hi, how are you?" So of course I couldn't work even in a café, even if I could speak the language a little.'

She chose instead to be a chambermaid in a small hotel. She had never cleaned rooms before, but this was her first foot on a ladder whose top was already in view. She took English courses, and proved a quick learner. She found that she enjoyed the work. 'I have always liked cleaning up at home—I like a clean house—so, you know, this kind of work, I suppose it made sense to me.'

She graduated from hotel rooms to private ones and got a job looking after a family in Epping Forest. Here she had her own room. Better still, 'the family was really nice.' After two years, she was promoted to personal assistant, helping the man of the house manage property. He had spotted Monika's potential. She soon found herself overseeing a total of 70 homes, preparing flats for new tenants when old tenants moved out, and arranging refurbishments when necessary. 'I have a good eye,' she says, allowing a slight smile.

Their relationship, she says, was always above board, explaining: 'I felt like his daughter.' When the family went on holiday to their villa in Spain, she went with them, both to look after the children and to top up her tan. 'I had plenty of free time.' She found that she liked the job, liked Epping Forest, and London in general.

'Oh, I absolutely love the English people.' In Slovakia, people don't know how to have half as much fun, she says. 'In a bank or a shop, you don't ask people: "How are you, how is your day?" If you do, they look at you like: "What do you want from me? You are a stranger! I don't know you. Don't talk to me!" I am sorry to say this, but they are miserable people. This is because, I think, the Slovakian mentality. It's very different.'

By comparison, Londoners were open and friendly. 'They know how to laugh. They know how to joke.'

I am speaking with Monika in the grand headquarters of

the agency that has matched her with wealthy individuals for the last few years. A manager called Arabella is responsible for finding Monika's placements. Like Monika, Arabella is elegant and discreet; she radiates much the same aura. When I ask Monika to tell me about her work as a domestic cleaner, Arabella immediately corrects my slip of the tongue.

'We don't say domestic cleaners. We say housekeepers.' She smiles encouragingly. 'I know it's just semantics, but the people we employ and the jobs they do—it's not like your average Mrs Mop, a typical char lady. And someone like Monika, especially. Monika has been a house manager for several years now. So while it's true to say that she may share many of the duties with the kind of cleaners you've been talking to, hers is a very different job, with much greater responsibility.'

After managing properties and working for what may have been one of the most generous families in the south-east of England, Monika was forced to find a new job when they moved to the north of England. Though she was terribly fond of them and wanted to follow them (they wanted her, too) she ultimately decided to remain south. She soon found employment elsewhere through Arabella—a job in Mayfair in a grand house owned by a grand Saudi family.

It is at this point that her poise slips slightly. When I ask her to recount her experiences here, she tells me that she doesn't want to come across as racist, because, she assures, she isn't. She is reluctant to sound as if she is stereotyping a nation, too. 'Not my intention,' she says, adding that there are good and bad people all over the world, and that she has worked for some English people who were also 'mean.' However, she found this particular Saudi family to be especially hard work.

'What I can say to you is that they are very demanding people, and that to look after them is a really, really difficult job.'

Arabella explains that Saudi Arabians are among the most demanding of employers. In their country, they often employ Indian or Filipino cleaners who are routinely expected to work seven days a week, 12 hours a day and more. The cleaners can only take holidays when the family is also on holiday. 'Such families often travel the world a lot, for work, but if they remain in one particular house for, say, eight months, then their staff will have to work for those eight months, every day.'

In Mayfair, where Monika was contracted (and paid) to work just five days a week and to commute to work like everybody else—she continued to live on the fringes of Essex, a good hour away on the Central line—she nevertheless soon found herself being called into work every day.

'I tried to explain to them about my contract, about my 40 hours a week, because that's what I was getting paid for. But I'm not sure if my boss understood, or, if she did, whether she wanted to understand. I had to explain to her that that was the law here, that that was how it works. If she wanted more from me, then we would have to sit down and agree on things. We would have to have new terms.'

Her employer was not going to discuss hours of work with an employee. She expected Monika to be both on-call and on-tap. When Monika was absent one Saturday morning, Arabella received an angry phone call asking where on earth she was. Arabella tells me that her work usually runs smoothly, because she has spent so many years building up good relationships with her global clients. She is a born diplomat and knows how to manage people—their expectations and temperaments. But, she admits, sometimes there are issues, often cultural ones. When Arabella politely explained Monika's contract to her Saudi employer, the client went temporarily deaf and then went on the offensive. The house in Mayfair was big, she complained. It needed constant care and attention.

Monika looks at me now, exasperated. 'It's a hard job, looking after such a big place. So you need some rest, right?'

A somewhat fractious compromise was agreed upon: Monika would work six days a week, with Sundays off. For five months in the house in Mayfair, she enjoyed just 15 minutes a day for lunch, indigestion a side effect of her work.

'I worked 12 hours a day, six days a week, in a house that had four bedrooms, four bathrooms, an entrance room, an office, three living rooms, kitchen, dining room, a bar in the basement.

And then there was the mews house that they also owned, which had two bedrooms, a laundry room, a washing room. I had to iron the clothes, and I had to help the chef in the kitchen. And let me tell you, chefs are very messy, the messiest people in the world, oh my God! When a chef cooks, everything is dirty, from floor to ceiling.'

It is not easy working for people whose financial disposition convinces them that they exist on elevated levels above everybody else. But it is possible. Vincent Vermeulen tells me that very often wealthy individuals behave the way they do for perfectly explicable reasons. 'You must understand the pressure they are under: with their work, their lives,' he says—and that it is entirely possible to have a functional and even pleasant professional union. These are people, he reiterates, who have so many demands made on their time that they sometimes overlook common courtesies. The more their staff facilitate the smooth running of the many moving parts that make up a typical working day, the more harmony there will be.

'In the last 30 to 40 years,' he says, 'people have realised that if you still try to treat your butlers like shit, then they will leave you. Simple as that. And what happens then? You have to look after yourself.' The average high net worth individual does not want to look after themselves. Many simply wouldn't know how. 'So what we are seeing increasingly is much more mutual respect between employer and employee. These are people who want stability, they want long-term. Yes, for sure, sometimes things will go wrong, and people won't be nice, but a lot of the time we have people staying in their jobs for years for the simple reason that it is a good one.'

Monika tells me that she enjoys her job despite its occasional trials. Mayfair was a blip, the Epping Forest family more the norm. She once worked for a princess of the Royal Family in Dubai, where she was every bit as invisible as her employer was to her. 'I didn't see her once. I entered the room to clean it after she had left it. When she returned, the room was clean—as if,' she laughs slyly, 'by magic.'

Monika will continue to operate at such altitude because she likes the wealthy world. It fascinates her. She likes the properties and likes to be part of it all, even if only by association. It's hard work, but rarely dull. 'And besides, I'm not afraid of hard work. I just want respect. And most times, I get it.'

One thing she hasn't experienced over her many years of working for such people is envy. The more she sees the impact riches can have on a person, the less she wants them for herself. It's destructive, she tells me, intrusive, and impacts on every area of life. It makes people miserable. Vincent Vermeulen agrees.

'Rich people, in my experience, get very bored,' he says. 'Do you know what they love more than anything else? A waiting list. They love to be on a waiting list!' This is because rich people can get whatever they want, whenever they want it, 'but to be put on a waiting list whets their appetite. It means there is something they want that they cannot have straight away, so of course they become crazy about it. They always want new things, special things: bigger yachts, faster cars, deeper basements.'

Of course, the moment they reach the top of the waiting list, and claim their prize, complacency swiftly reasserts itself and they seek out the next thing to crave. This way madness lies.

Vermeulen says that some people he works with, predominantly women, and predominantly from eastern Europe, choose this type of work in the hope of ensnaring a principal for themselves. They want to replace the wife. It's a fanciful fantasy, this, a bit like buying lottery tickets. But, as with lottery tickets, sometimes the numbers do come up.

'On more than one occasion, I've been called by someone I previously trained to tell me that they have been promoted, with benefits! They have become the new Lady of the House, and that they want me to send them a new housemaid!' Vermeulen is ready to help. 'I will always have more recently-graduated housemaids to offer,' he points out.

Monika has yet to have an affair with one of her principals, and insists that it will never happen. 'This is not why I got into this work,' she tells me firmly. On two occasions, she does admit that she has been turned down for jobs because she was deemed to be 'too beautiful,' and therefore constituted a risk. 'I wanted to explain that I wasn't here to turn out the wife, that I respected them, and that I valued the job, and also my reputation. I have no interest in a relationship with anyone I work with. I'm in this job because I like to work with people, I like working with important people, and I like helping to run important, busy households.'

She knows her boundaries, she says. 'This is a good job. I have no desire to leave it.'

13. The Listener

For the past 14 years, Jennifer has been living 6,000 miles from home. She currently shares a small flat in Shepherd's Bush with two other Filipino women, both also cleaners. She herself has been cleaning houses across London—in Wimbledon, Hampstead, Golders Green and, she says, 'anywhere there is a job'—six days a week, year after year. Jennifer is 43 and speaks perfect English. She is highly educated. Back home in the Philippines, she trained as a teacher, then worked as a travel agent. The story she tells is a familiar one.

'I didn't make enough money there, and certainly not enough to look after my daughters. I had to come here.'

She has worked in nursing homes, but not right now. 'My visa expired, and I didn't want to get [the care home] in trouble,' she says. I ask if this means that she is no longer in the UK legally. Her smile is hesitant. 'I'm not sure.'

Like so many of the domestic helps I speak to, Jennifer has grudgingly become accustomed to her work. 'At first it was a little bit depressing, of course, but then eventually, you know...' A shrug renders further explanation unnecessary. 'It's my job. I earn money. I send money back home to my family.'

She no longer focuses on the drudgery, but gets on and does what needs to be done. In every house, she says, that would be something different. Sometimes she is employed simply to clean. Sometimes she is asked to iron, too. The children are not part of her duties, except when they are—'because I have been asked to look after them, or to cook for them from time to time, and I don't like to tell them "no."' She says: 'When the mothers ask, it's hard to turn them down. They will say to me: *I have to go out, can you take care of my daughter?* How can I refuse?'

Crossing her arms, she continues. 'They take you for granted, these people, definitely.' This is why she now attends the Sunday meetings of The Voice of Domestic Workers. 'You have to know your rights.'

On average she will clean at least three houses a day, sometimes for up to four or five hours per house. The days are long. She works by herself, and for herself, no agency, and makes on average £10 an hour. Because she is so willing, and because the distances between the houses she cleans are so great, a significant chunk of her earnings goes on topping up her Oyster card.

Jennifer is personable, friendly and open. She has a broad, intelligent face; the ponytail gives her a youthful air, and she smiles quickly. She does not look downtrodden. Easy to talk to, she gives the impression of being a good listener. She tells me that her clients often think of her so. Perhaps this is why she has become like a psychoanalyst to some. 'They see me as a shoulder to cry on, perhaps?'

She tells me about a single woman, in her mid-fifties, who lives in a red brick house in upmarket Belsize Park, on one of those languorous avenues where trees on either side of the street arc to meet one another in the middle. This woman's private life seems to be a disaster, and that disaster finds its expression in every room of her house. The place, Jennifer says, 'is horrible, just horrible. So messy. For example, she has a dishwasher, yes? But does she ever put the plates in there? Everything is in the sink, just piling up. You don't know where to start. Cleaning that place, it's very difficult for me! It makes me just think: Oh. My. God!'

The woman was sad and lonely, angry too. 'Her mess was like an expression of her pain, I think.' Jennifer developed a better understanding when she started to clean for the woman's father, who lived further up the hill, towards Hampstead Heath. He quickly took Jennifer into his confidence, telling her about each of the children he'd had, and that this particular daughter had always been the chaotic one.

'So some things don't change,' Jennifer pronounces. 'She is always on the phone, this woman, always talking, and always pacing while she is talking. Whatever is going on on the phone— it's high drama, you know?' And while she talks, and paces, she upsets the harmony that Jennifer has just tried so hard to reassert.

'She just walks up and down, never relaxes. But then I think, she can't. For her, to relax, to breathe... it's impossible.' It would be easier for Jennifer to clean if the woman were absent. 'But she never is.'

This particular woman isn't a rarity, a one-off. Others also conduct their private lives publicly while Jennifer tries, sometimes in vain, to clean. She is telling me now of another woman who manages to create a mess while Jennifer tidies up. Jennifer will finish the kitchen and move on to the bedroom, but by the time she has finished in the bedroom and returns to the kitchen, it has reverted to its disaster zone status. Instinctively, Jennifer wants to clean it up again, but she is paid only by the hour, so the only way she can finish is to ignore the trail left in her wake. Then, when she is ready to leave, and to be paid, politely saying to the lady: 'Okay, I'm done, goodbye, see you next time,' the lady will look up, in all innocence until the innocence turns to fury. 'But the kitchen!' she tells Jennifer. 'Look! It's still so incredibly messy!'

At this point Jennifer has to remind herself not to blow up, not to answer back. 'I just want to say to her: Oh my God! I just cleaned it up, just now! You saw me! You—you!—were the one to mess it up again, and I'm sorry, but I just don't have time to clean it up again, not now.'

Instead, she swallows the rebuke and takes a deep breath. She leaves, politely but firmly closing the door behind her. But a sense of anxiety weighs heavily on her shoulders for the rest of the day, the knowledge that she has left someone angry when she wanted to leave them satisfied. 'It's hard, you know?'

Jennifer says that sometimes these ladies, who live on their own, have problems that she recognises and empathises with. They might be single when they want to be married, they might be lonely. Many are elderly, and have lost spouses. 'These people, they don't throw things away. They—what's the word…? Hoarding. They hoard everything. So much clutter. Perhaps they like it? Maybe I am thinking that their problems are psychological. But I can't deal with their psychological problems, I can only tidy up after them. So when they make a mess as soon as I am tidying up, it's difficult not to get angry. I have to say to them: "Sorry, but this is not my fault, madam. I clean your house, but I do it once. If you make another mess while I am still cleaning, then I have to do extra, and extra, and extra. And you don't pay me more. It isn't fair."'

Frowning, she adds: 'Sometimes, I get very annoyed.'

There's the woman who claims to suffer with OCD. 'But I don't believe her. I think it's just an excuse for her to hurt people, because that's all she does. She shouts all the time. OCD doesn't mean that you are nasty to people all the time, I think. She shouts at me, at her family members. It's horrible.'

And yet, I say, she goes back week after week? Sighing, she tells me that, yes, she does. The previous cleaner had been frightened off by the client, she says. 'I took on the job because of the money. The woman had told me that she wanted me to come every day, and I knew that this would be good money, of course. But after all the shouting? To be honest with you, I couldn't do it. So I told her I could only do one day a week.

'This woman, she wants me to feed her children as well as clean. She gets me to clean up the entire house, and keeps me there until her children come home, and then she asks me to make them something to eat. I ask her what, and she pulls out a whole chicken from the fridge. "Here," she says to me. "Roast this." I tell her: "Madam, I've just finished cleaning. I have to go to my next job now, so I have no time. Forgive me."'

On this particular occasion, Jennifer left, and her day continued. She got home, habitually exhausted, at nine o'clock. She sat with her flatmates over a late dinner, the television on. Half an hour later, the phone rang. It was the OCD lady, calling belatedly to remonstrate. 'I picked up my phone, said hello, and she was shouting already, just shouting. She wanted to know why I didn't roast the chicken, why I left her children hungry.' This time, Jennifer says, her instinctive diplomacy flew out the window. 'I told her that she could not do this to me. She could not call me this late at night and shout at me. I told her that I was a person just like she was, that I had feelings too. Your behaviour, I told her, is not right.'

Every person is different, Jennifer concedes, 'but there is always something.' When I ask the worst part of the job, she answers, simply: being taken advantage of. She gets booked for three hours, and is expected to do four. She doesn't have to look after the children but making them dinner every night would be ever so appreciated. The pile of clothes she isn't required to iron, but it would be great if she did all the same.

'I take pride in my job, I'm that type of person. If I'm not sure I've done a good job in a house, I have to go back, even if it's on my own time, just to make sure. It stays on my mind. I need to make sure I did it right. I like to see a place sparkling clean when I go. I can be very proud of what I've done. It's nice that it smells good, that it looks clean. It's nice when an employer refers me to one of their friends, because it means I have done a good job, and that job has been noticed.'

I ask whether it pays enough, and she nods. 'I can say that, yes, it does, when I am paid by the hour, and not expected to do more, for free.'

Jennifer is also a licensed massage therapist. She prefers being a masseur to cleaning, but so far she has been able to find more dirty kitchens than bad backs. But she still practises whenever she can. Her daughters back in the Philippines appreciate the extra money. Because of her day job, her massage appointments tend to be at night. Often she is too tired, but will still go whenever she is called. 'I massage people at 10 o'clock at night sometimes,' she says. 'They rely on me. I don't want to let them down.'

Sometimes, her clients pursue her in her dreams. She dreams about one particular employer, a Chinese lady, who likes to follow her around the house putting two fingers to every surface she has just dusted to see if any motes remain. The Chinese lady is persistent in her efforts. There is a piano in this house, and Jennifer cleans all 88 keys, keenly aware that the lady will come and run her finger along each one of them in turn, playing as she does her own sonata of pedantic exactitude.

Jennifer laughs sourly. 'She makes me so stressed, she gives me nightmares. I keep waiting for her to call me back, to tell me that maybe I didn't do something properly, that I missed something. So far, it all seems okay, and I sigh with relief because I am happy, but do you know what? My heart. My heart is racing all the time.'

When she was still living in the Philippines, it was a dream for her to come to somewhere like London. She knew of many Filipinos who left their country for work, and England was always the prime location, London in particular, the haven they were seeking. Domestic work is riven with stories of abuse at the hands of merciless clients, and complicated cultural ideals, but in London, the Filipinos believe, there will be salvation of sorts.

'It is definitely better here, I can say that,' Jennifer says, 'but not all white people are good. And when bad things happen, I suppose it can change the way you look at individuals, and cultures. I've heard so many stories of people being mistreated, and like I have told you, so many people here have psychological issues. They use the psychological issues to stamp on you.' She means this metaphorically, I hope. 'I'll be honest with you. Sometimes I feel that I've had enough of it, and part of my brain has to tell the other part: calm down, calm down. The only consolation of this job is that you have money. You don't particularly like the job, but you get paid to do it, so you can send money home. If you are physically abused, or emotionally, or whatever, you have to take it. Your family expects.'

Her daily mantra is this: 'At the end of the week, I have my money.'

I ask her how she relaxes, how she enjoys herself in her adopted home of 14 years. She tells me that she rarely goes out to eat, or the cinema, and that if she is feeling particularly in need of a treat, she will get herself a flat white. 'I like flat whites, good coffee,' she says, 'but expensive, so I have no more than two a week.'

She has met many of the south-east Asian diaspora at The Voice of Domestic Workers, and the social aspect of the group has given a new shape to her sometimes empty, lonely days off. 'There is a community here, which I like. It's nice to be busy on Sundays, on the days I don't work. It means it's not too depressing.'

She is not currently in a relationship. 'No time!' But finding a way out of the monotony of her working week is essential. 'I've noticed that a lot of people who come here on Sundays still don't know how to talk about their personal situations. They keep to themselves. They don't know how to let it out, they are not yet willing to share. I was like that once. It takes time to open up, and to talk about what life is like here, and how perhaps it could be better.'

Had she never left her birth country, she might have remained a teacher, she believes, a high school teacher preparing the next generation for life. Instead, she is thousands of miles from home, approaching her middle years, and sharing a flat with two other women with whom, she admits, she sometimes fights. 'But, you know, it's okay.'

London has become her home. 'Life in the fast lane!' she jokes. 'I think I would be lost if I returned back to Manila. I'm not Filipino any more. I'm British. That's how I think of myself.'

This doesn't stop her from dreaming, however. Dreaming costs nothing.

'Sometimes I think to myself: when will I do something in life that I really love? Because, I have to tell you, cleaning is not something I love. It's something I do.'

So what's the answer? She looks to an indeterminate point beyond my shoulder, and the smile that spreads across her face is a faraway one, untethered to her mouth. Quickly, it fades.

'Maybe one day I'll find it,' she says, shrugging. 'Maybe. I hope.'

14. The Gay Cleaner

When women clean without their clothes on, there exists a curious rectitude. When men do, it's open season. Anything can happen. And sometimes does.

A certain sense of world-weariness settles about Felipe's shoulders that prompts both empathy and then, later, sympathy. He seems put upon, and occasionally sick of it all. Felipe is aged 38 and a Colombian resident of London. He is slim and compact, with sharp cheekbones and a kind, mournful expression. He has been advertising himself online for a few months as a 'gay-friendly cleaner,' and is now living with the consequences. In the ad, it suggests that he is 'an experienced and efficient cleaner providing services to both domestic and corporate clients.' His services include 'ironing, washing and general cleaning. I can do domestic cleaning, one-off cleanings, before and after party cleaning, tenancy cleaning, office cleaning and spring cleaning.'

He is, he suggests, 'efficient, reliable, trustworthy, extremely tidy and organised, friendly, hard-working, energetic and a good timekeeper. I will,' he stresses, 'always be on time.' The picture that accompanies the text is of Felipe in a dress shirt and bow tie. He looks terribly smart.

When I first read the words 'gay-friendly,' I thought it must be a kind of code for something. Perhaps Felipe was really an escort, and the suggestion of him being a good cleaner was merely a ruse. But, he tells me both patiently and impatiently, that is not the case. I'm not the only person to read innuendo into his description.

He says sadly: 'Happens all the time.' But then he believes this is typical of a certain kind of gay man, a predator always on the prowl, the sort who reads into things whatever he wants to for the sole reason that he craves it. The internet is a time waster's paradise. We click and we click, alighting for a second or two on anything that might catch our eye, before we get bored and move on elsewhere, to the next page and the page after that. Felipe has received no end of cursory enquiries from potential customers that never went anywhere and many others from people who had thought—hoped—he offered rather more than that.

The reason he labelled himself 'gay friendly,' he tells me, was not just to reach his nominal target audience of gay men with houses to clean, but also because he is gay and friendly.

'So maybe this way, I meet nice people, I work for nice people, and I make friends. Who knows?'

When I hear his stories, Felipe is still comparatively new to advertising online, but he is learning quickly. In his experience, men by their very nature are predatory and not necessarily to be trusted. We meet in a train station pub in the early afternoon that is empty save for middle-of-the-day drinkers who sit at perimeter tables and clutch their pints so tightly their knuckles turn white. Felipe orders a cappuccino that comes served in a large cup that seems to be comprised largely of chocolate-dusted foam.

He tells me that he finds it increasingly hard to inhabit London's gay world. 'People, they take advantage of you all the time.' He's been the victim of some bad experiences over the past few years, partners using drugs in his company, telling him they loved him but then treating him badly, taking things from him, stealing, occasionally leaving him in debt. 'It's become quite tough, the gay scene here. I'm not sure why. I don't know why these people tell me that they are kind, only to then take from me, but it's not a good situation. Sometimes I just want to go back home to Colombia, or perhaps Venezuela, where I spent some of my childhood. It's difficult here, very stressful. I think there would be more tranquillity at home.'

When we meet, Venezuela is mired in political chaos. People are fleeing towards its borders in the hope of escaping. Would it really be more tranquil for Felipe there than in London? Slowly, perhaps grimly, he nods his head. 'I think so, yes. I'm tired of all this.'

He tells me about his current partner at length, and I say that he, the partner, sounds feckless and irresponsible, even juvenile and immature. 'Yes, but he is 56, so he's not about to grow out of it any time soon.'

Felipe followed his Colombian boyfriend to London, arriving in 1999. Born and raised in Colombia, he spent several years in Venezuela before returning to Bogotá as a teenager. He liked it in Bogotá, though things were difficult for homosexuals. He had to keep his sexuality a secret. 'I lost one job there when they discovered I was gay.' By comparison London felt like an enveloping hug. He had his boyfriend and they were out all the time at parties, clubs. He lost count of the amount of Sunday dawns he saw in, radiant and happy on the capital's rain-slicked city streets.

After two years, he and his partner broke up, but he was settled by then. He has lived in Maida Vale, the Isle of Dogs, then Croydon. London is home. He got a job in a wine shop in Shoreditch and rose to assistant manager. The job lasted several years, but after some staff restructuring, he lost his position. He had to find something else and ended up working at a bed and breakfast in the centre of the city.

'A gay bed and breakfast.'

Things became complicated. He was often the victim of unwanted approaches. 'My boss...' he says, before trailing off. The longer we talk, and the more Felipe becomes uncomfortable talking, the more guilty I feel for making him discuss something that clearly discomfits him. 'I'm fine,' he says.

In the B&B, he did a little of everything. He cleaned the rooms, made breakfast, did the ironing. He frequently ironed for his boss, too. Occasionally, his boss would ask him whether he might consider doing so naked, just for the fun of it, because why not, where's the harm? Felipe was reluctant, but couldn't lose the job. 'I ended up saying yes and I did it for him on three occasions.' Duly encouraged, his boss—who tended to walk about the place unclothed—also asked him to give him massages. The muscles in his back were tight. He craved release. 'But he thought the massages were sexual. For me they were not.'

When I ask Felipe why he did this—because this isn't a practice you'd necessarily find at a Premier Inn—and whether it was a shortcut to becoming intimate with residents, Felipe nods. 'Well, if they were up for it, then, yes, I suppose so.' And were some of them up for it? 'Yes.'

The third and final time Felipe found himself ironing naked, his boss took a very determined step towards him. 'He asked me to do something really—' He blanches, then reaches into his bag to make sure that his mobile phone is switched off, fearful somebody may be listening in. 'Well, it was rude, and I just lost it. I left.'

It was then that he decided to work for himself, on his own terms. He advertised himself as a 'gay-friendly' cleaner.

As he starts to explain, he plays with the spoon in his saucer and wipes off some errant foam. 'No offence, but I never used to clean for straight people. Do you want to know why?' He starts to grin. 'It is because, for me, I found that straight people are so much more untidy than gay people. They are just not as clean! Gay people, they tend to be cleaner.' He holds his hands up in front of him as if expecting reproach. 'This is what I have seen! Gay men tidy up after themselves, but straight people? And women in particular? So untidy!' He laughs, then adds: 'Sooo untidy! This is my experience anyway, you know?'

His first clients were straight: a family of four in Croydon. 'I thought, okay, I will go to meet them, but I did have a feeling as soon as I walked through the front door that this wasn't going to be for me. But then they turned out to be lovely people and I found that I didn't particularly mind the mess. So that's why I stayed with them: they were nice to me. But, oh, when I first saw their house—it was completely upside down!'

He still cleans for them. Visiting their home for two hours per visit, it takes him three days to spruce up the place. As a comparison, the single gay man he cleans for once a week in

Clapham takes just a couple of hours. 'It's physical work, with the family, but at least I am busy, and I do like being busy.'

He points out that not every gay man who books him is a sexual predator. Most treat him well, like a peer, someone with feelings, just like them. 'With some of my clients, we have become friends, gone out for dinner together, to the theatre, the cinema. One is taking me to the Royal Festival Hall soon to see a classical concert.' When things like this happen, it restores his faith in both men and human beings in general. He likes it when people see the person behind the cleaner. In Colombia, he says, it isn't always like this.

'I did a bit of cleaning in Bogotá years ago, and I was treated very badly there. People shouted at me all the time.' He recounts three sisters who treated him like something they had stepped in and were keen to scrub off. He once spoke to one of the sisters, in Spanish, using the informal 'you' (tu) instead of its more formal counterpart (usted). 'She shouted at me, and told me to never talk to her like that again, that I was nobody, merely her worker, and, she said: "Don't you forget it!"' He slumps in his seat. 'As a cleaner, you are always going to be lower class in Colombia than anyone else. In London, not so much.'

This doesn't mean he always advertises his profession to the men he dates. When hooking up with potential partners, he'll try to avoid the subject of work. 'Prospective boyfriends, they become less interested when they learn you are a cleaner, this is what I find. They just won't bother going out with you at all. I suppose it's not an industry that brings respect. But mostly people are much nicer to me here than they are back in South America.'

He says that he likes the job, mostly, and that though he craves a return to the wine industry, cleaning is flexible, it pays well enough, and he is pretty much his own boss. But Felipe, as a sensitive man, is frequently embarrassed by what he finds in homes and wishes people would be more discreet. Many of his clients don't bother to conceal private items before he arrives, things that Felipe would really rather not see at all—much less wipe down and secrete away in bedside drawers. He becomes uncomfortable when we broach this subject. Are we talking about sex toys, I ask?

He says nothing for a few moments. 'Oh dear, well, I don't know how to say it but—it's terrible, really.' What is, I ask him? 'These huge... I mean, huge—' Toys? 'So big. What do you do with them, because I just don't know...'

Felipe feels that making an unmade bed is one thing, decluttering it of sex dungeon paraphernalia quite another. Anyway, he says, metaphorically brushing all this to one side, such displays are the exception, not the norm. Most clients are nice, approachable people who very often just want to have a connection with someone who happens to be 'gay' and 'friendly.'

'I love it when I become friends with my clients. And it does happen. I clean up for them, and then they invite me to stay afterwards, to have lunch with them, a glass of wine. That's when I really like the job. I like it less when I have to remind people that I am not a prostitute, that I am not there to have sex with them, or even to go out on dates with them if I don't want to, but just to clean. I am a good cleaner, you know?' He looks almost wistful now. 'I wish I didn't have to remind people about this so many times, but I do.'

Epilogue. Clocking Off

Once Boglárka has removed all traces of infidelity from the first house of the day and reimposed its order, so that the returning wife, when she returns later in the week, will know nothing, she closes the front door behind her, locks it, and places the keys in their pocket in her handbag, separate from all the other keys to all the other houses that live within their own compartments, and goes on her way.

It is almost 11 o'clock in the morning, and the weather, the 'shitty English weather,' as she puts it, is living up to expectation. 'It always rains, it's always cold.' She pulls the hood up on her coat, unchains her bicycle and cycles the half mile to the tube station. Her next house is two travel zones away, too far for the bike.

'Okay, so it takes half an hour by tube, or a whole hour by bus,' she tells me. 'This is what I have to figure out every day: how far my next house is and how I can get there quick. But the bus is cheaper, I have time, so I take the bus.'

She chains her bike to a lamppost, then crosses the road and waits by the bus stop. 'My whole life,' she laughs, 'waiting for the bloody bus.'

Every seven to nine minutes, the timetable promises. She waits almost 20. While she waits, cold and wet and shivering, she realises that she could murder a Starbucks latte, 'but it is Monday today, and I don't have my Starbucks until Wednesday.' Instead, she makes do with a swig from a bottle of water bought earlier from the local Co-op, and a packet of ready salted crisps. As her fingers near her mouth, she can smell the sharp tang of household bleach. She pulls something from her pocket. 'This is why I carry these,' she says, retrieving a small pack of wet wipes with a citrus scent.

Boglárka arrives at the next house a quarter of an hour late. It's empty, and for this she offers a silent prayer of thanks. 'Always easier this way, nobody home.' She takes off her coat in the hallway, and her Nikes, and changes them for house shoes, then appraises the damage: three bedrooms, three unmade beds, a pile of breakfast dishes in the sink, cat hair on the sofa, the bathroom grimed with tidemarks the colour of nicotine. The television in the living room is on, competing with the radio in the parents' bedroom. She switches both off.

'I like my music when I work. Everything else is just noise, you know?'

But in the kids' room, the Xbox is still alive on the wall-mounted TV, replaying the cacophonous menu page for a war game featuring men with outsized biceps cradling machine guns, with hand grenades strapped to their belts. 'I can never work out how to turn off their TV,' she says, 'so in this house, I bring my earphones.'

The carpet in this room is almost entirely concealed beneath a pile of clothes belonging to the two boys, 12 and 14 respectively. 'The dangerous years,' she jokes. She never knows which are clean, and which are dirty, which she needs to fold and put back in the wardrobe, which she needs to tip into the washing machine. She recalls the time, in another house, she picked up a man's suit from the floor of the bedroom and put it into the washing machine, added washing powder, switched it on, and thought nothing more of it.

'The man call me later to tell me I ruin his suit. He sacked me.'

So now she proceeds with care. Smelling the discarded clothes of prepubescent boys to determine their cleanliness is not the highlight of her day.

When, two hours later, she arrives into the kitchen, she vacuums, mops, polishes, waxes and dusts. She transfers the dirty plates and bowls to the dishwasher, and washes away the grease splats from the splashback. She picks up the litre of milk that has been left on the kitchen table—by one of the boys, no doubt—sniffs it first to ensure it's not gone off, then puts it back in the fridge. On the fridge's second shelf she sees a bowl, wrapped in clingfilm. Affixed to it is a Post-it note which says: 'Boglárka, for you, if you're hungry.' It's a little after one o'clock. She is hungry. She had been planning to stop off at another Co-op on the way to her next appointment for a cheese sandwich, reliably the cheapest thing on the shelf, so she finds herself inordinately grateful for the thoughtfulness extended here, not the first time from this particular woman, whom she has only met once.

'These are small kindnesses, you know?' she says. 'But they make my day.'

She sends another silent prayer upwards.

She sits now at the gleaming kitchen counter on one of the high stools, and unwraps the bowl, reaching for a fork from the cutlery drawer. What little she knows of this family can be surmised from the contents of the fridge, much of which is gluten- and lactose-free. The vegetable compartment is full with green stuff. In previous weeks, she has filed away epi pens and insulin pumps into bedside drawers and rearranged an array of complicated vitamins and supplements in their kitchen and bathroom cabinets.

In the bowl there is farro or possibly spelt, she can never quite tell, along with kidney beans, rectangles of avocado and tiny sprigs of broccoli. 'It has vinegar in it, and these big flakes of salt, and it's good! Better than what I make for myself at home, you know?'

She eats quickly, both aware that she is in someone else's kitchen and shouldn't get too comfortable, and also that it is 1.15pm; she has to be at her next job, across town, within the hour.

She finishes, washes the bowl and fork, dries both, and puts them back in their respective cupboards. She takes a swig from the Co-op water bottle in her bag, then finds the Post-it notes, and a pen, and writes 'thank u,' which she leaves on the now spotless kitchen counter. She closes and locks the front door behind her. She is running 20 minutes late. She goes by bus.

'I like taking the bus sometimes,' she says. 'You see British people up close, and you talk to them.' Here she sits, on the lower deck, not the upper—she's no fool—alongside the elderly and the long-term unemployed. Some talk to her about politics, about Brexit. Occasionally, she has borne the brunt of their abuse. 'Go home,' she has been told on more than one occasion, to which she has always wanted to respond (but hasn't): 'What, to Streatham?' But she knows what they mean. She is different, foreign. A job-snatcher, a benefits cheat.

'But what I wonder is, these people, they rely on us, no? They rely on us to tidy up after them, to repair their houses...'

If she and her kind really did all pack up and go home, who would do what she does day in and day out, for the minimum wage?

'I want to say to people: I contribute to society just like you do, you know?'

From 2.30pm until 4.30pm, Boglárka cleans a tall, angular flat whose spiral staircase makes it difficult to transport the vacuum cleaner from floor to floor. 'Careful you don't chip the woodwork,' was what the owner told her when they first met. He lives alone, this man, no pets but many, many pot plants, the kind that are perched on mantelpieces and high window ledges, whose leaves droop low like entrails.

'Let me tell you, he loves his plants,' Boglárka says. 'He tells me to wipe the dust from the leaves, but never to water the soil. Only he can feed his plants. This is fine by me.'

While she gets on with her work here, she plugs into more music on her six-year-old Samsung with its cracked screen. She listens to Yonderboi, Tankcsapda, and to Celine Dion and Mariah Carey. Like Celine, she finds that her heart will go on.

From 5.15pm until eight, she tunes into Radio 4 while cleaning the rambling house of an elderly couple who don't leave cellophaned bowls of health food for her in the fridge. But they are present throughout her visit and ply her with cups of sugary tea and digestive biscuits. These will tide her over until she gets home. The tea begins to press on her after a while. But, she says: 'I don't like going in someone else's house when they are in it.' So she holds it in as best she can, half convincing herself that while she dusts around them, they can hear the PG Tips in her bladder sloshing about.

By 8.15pm, 12 hours since her first job, she is done for the day, on the tube—'expensive but fast—necessary!'—back to her bike, which is still there waiting for her, locked against the lamppost. She fishes out her front and back lights from her bag, then puts on her helmet. While she cycles the final three miles home, she begins to realise just how hungry the physical labour has made her.

'I don't eat a lot during the day, too busy, too expensive,' she says, 'so when I get home, oh boy, I need to eat!'

Home is a shared fourth floor flat in Streatham, with two other eastern European women, also cleaners. They rent, and have never met the landlord. 'It is not so nice, but it is okay,' she says. The toilet has a habit of gurgling all night if flushed after 9pm, so wherever possible they try to avoid late-night flushes.

The first thing she does when she gets home is to go into her room, and collapse onto her pull-out bed, groaning theatrically and swearing in her native tongue. Her flatmates are in the kitchen, taking turns at the microwave. She shouts at them to fetch her lasagne from the freezer while she nips to the bathroom to relieve her bladder, brush her teeth and have a quick but thorough shower.

They eat around their tiny uneven formica table, a wad of Starbucks napkins sellotaped at the base of one of the legs for parity, clinking beer bottles together and recounting tales about their day. And then each of them retreat to the balcony to smoke, looking out at the city streets beneath them with their neon-lit takeaways, buzzing mopeds and police sirens. 'Always, the police sirens.'

At 10 o'clock, 11 o'clock back home, she Skypes her sullen teenage daughter, who otherwise insists that she is fine and happy, and that grandma and grandpa are treating her well.

'I miss her, you know?' Boglárka says to me. 'I see that she has lost weight, but I can't say this to her because she will get angry with me, so all I can say to her is: "I'm thinking of you."'

And what does her daughter say in reply?

'"Yes, Mama," is what she tells me. And then she passes laptop to my mother and I speak to her for a while. I can see my father in the background, watching football match on television. I shout and wave at him and this is how we communicate: on computer.'

She tells me that she visits once, maybe twice a year, always by bus, which takes 30 hours, 'but it's worth it because it will take me all the way to Budapest; home.' But like so many people who leave their countries of origin only to return sporadically, home has become a complicated place. At first her mother will spoil her, as she always does, with a feast: goulash, lángos and főzelék, and for a while she will feel like weeping with pure joy at being surrounded by such familiar comforts.

But then the usual frustrations will start to seep in. A few days before she is due to return to London, her father will stop talking to her, while her mother will begin to openly snipe.

'She says I look tired, not taking care of myself. She reminds me my marriage broke up, and that I have left them both to look after my daughter, but they are old. This should be my job. This is always difficult for me. I feel guilty, but I have to say to her that I didn't leave for no reason; I left for money, opportunity. I tell her again and again that there is work in London, much more than there ever was in Budapest. I haven't gone far away from home for the fun of it. This is what I tell her.'

But she's not sure she means this any more.

'Sometimes I think that, after six years, Budapest is not my home now. London is my home. When I go back, I am claustrophobic. It doesn't feel the same place, or maybe I don't feel the same. Who knows?'

So instead she looks to the future. In four years, her daughter will have finished school. She can come and join her then. They can be in the capital together, and start over.

Until then, she finds that she has grown unexpectedly accustomed to life in this foreign metropolis, to cleaning up after its natives. Her flatmates, bruised and world-weary, are her family now, and they bond like soldiers, fighting for a common cause, hunkered down together no matter what. They laugh nightly over cigarettes and beer while they ponder what they might do next in this global city that seems, at least on its shimmering surface, to promise so much.

'We could maybe start a nannying service, or dog walking,' she says. 'Londoners like their dogs, and they pay a lot! Sometimes we think we set up our own cleaning company, and then franchise it. I know people who have done this. They have websites, and everything.'

They fantasise about moving to a bigger flat, exchanging Streatham for Wandsworth, even the fringes of Battersea. They could become contestants on a reality TV show, then sell their stories to the papers. Giggling, they suggest that they could become babes on the *Babestation* TV channel. They could find rich husbands, who spoil them and send them to spas and nail salons and wellness centres.

They could club together and buy a Prius, and start working shifts for Uber. They could buy bikes and do Deliveroo on the side. They could perfect their English and teach other newcomers, or they could use it to get proper jobs: teachers, social workers, lawyers. Why not?

Or they could write. They could write about all their adventures here. The people they've met, the stories they've had to listen to, the many confounding things they get to see that take place behind the closed doors of crazy people who otherwise appear so prim and proper and sane. They could give an insight into what goes on in the privacy of their homes: the single women with their multiple neuroses; the married couples who are falling apart spectacularly; the families with far too many children and too many pets, and who live in chaos—all these curiously idiosyncratic ways in which people go about their complicated lives.

They could write about how they are taken advantage of. They could write about the connections they have made, the unlikely friendships, all the genuinely lovely individuals they have met, and those myriad examples of tiny daily kindnesses that mean so much.

And they could write about the men, too, the men who find themselves so unexpectedly aroused by their very presence, who always seem to be just coming out of the en-suite shower when they arrive in their bedrooms with the Hoover...

As their cigarette smoke intermingles in the air around them, four flights above the streets of Streatham during a brief lull in the rain on a crisp, cold Monday night, the women howl with laughter.

They like to hatch plans like this, to scheme and dream. Dreaming is free.

Afterword

It was about a decade ago when I first found myself employing the services of a domestic cleaner, a position I never thought I'd be in. I'd grown up in a single-parent family on a council estate in Peckham, with an obsessively houseproud mother of Yugoslav/Italian extraction who had neither the funds nor the inclination to ever employ someone else to do her dirty work. But now that I was a father of two, and my wife and I were working long hours, tidying up began to get away from us. We'd find better ways to spend our weekends, and so increasingly we were living in filth. I'd overheard mothers at the school gate talking about their cleaners, and I knew that these were people who couldn't necessarily afford hired help any more than we could but who made the necessary financial arrangements regardless. And so, self-conscious over this momentously middle-class step we were about to take, I asked around.

Turns out we were spoilt for choice, for there were many cleaners operating within our neighbourhood. I put in an enquiry, and the following Wednesday morning, shortly after my wife left for work, our very first cleaner arrived: Dena.

Dena was Romanian, late twenties, slim, with sharp cheekbones and a penetrating gaze, a Samsung rammed tight into one jeans pocket, a packet of cigarettes crushed inside the other. She worked her first shift quickly and efficiently, but in subsequent weeks seemed keen to linger longer over the coffee I offered her—and biscuits too—in order to chat. She told me about her life back in Romania, how she was the former wife of one of her country's biggest rap stars, and mother to his young daughter. 'He's very famous,' she told me. 'You have heard of him, I think.' I hadn't.

He was in 'beef' with other eastern European rappers, and had found it necessary to carry a gun, and to employ bodyguards. He had frequent affairs. For a while Dena tried to put up with his behaviour, until she didn't.

'I left him, and come to this country. Fresh start.'

Was her daughter with her, I wondered?

'No, no. My daughter back home, with him.' She paused. 'It's complicated.'

Over the next few months, Dena would contrive to find more time to talk, and less to clean. The house did not benefit from her scant efforts. She once caused a flood in the bathroom while trying to unclog the sink, and had her plumber flatmate come to fix it on the understanding that I would pay him for his trouble. Increasingly, she didn't bother turning up at all, sending her younger sister—a more recent arrival into the UK, with no word of English—in her stead. She began complaining about her other clients, these strange British families with their unusual habits and behaviours.

'I do not do this job for very long, I think,' she told me once. 'I have plans.'

I found myself helplessly intrigued by Dena, captivated by the stories she spun, and the life she was currently living. The migrant experience has always fascinated me. My mother had pursued her own version of it back in the 1960s as, decades later, my Spanish wife would, too.

I wanted to talk to people like Dena, and learn about their circumstances: what had brought them here in the first place, and what life was like far from home. Did they enjoy the work, or hate it? And what was their take on us, their British employers?

I thought I might write on the subject at some point but did nothing about it until one day, in late 2018, the publisher of Canbury Press, Martin Hickman, told me he had an idea for a book, and wondered whether I might like to have a crack at it: investigating the hidden lives of our domestic cleaners. A nice coincidence, I thought. Martin didn't have to ask twice, and I'm very grateful he gave me the opportunity.

It is not easy approaching those who normally live their lives under the radar, in the hope of asking them intrusive questions. I approached dozens of cleaning companies, and over 100 individual cleaners, who advertised their services online or, in some cases, in the windows of corner shops and local post offices. Some responded with initial interest, only to then ghost me. Others agreed to see me, but failed to show up at the designated time and place. Quite a few whom I did manage to meet then fell mute in my company, reasonably wary of this stranger with the notepad and dictaphone. One or two thought I was from the tax office, or else some other shadowy corner of the civil service, and that my intentions were not as innocent as initially advertised. Some wanted paying, those in the midst of already complicated lives for whom my request—which I had tried to make politely, with sensitivity—was just another unwanted intrusion.

One particular man, for example, cancelled our scheduled appointment because he was awaiting test results for cancer, and needed an operation on his knee, a work injury for which he was suing his employer. 'I'm absolutely fuming as it's the small man against the rich,' he texted. 'I am so mad because my injury has ruined my happiness and made me realise when u rely on your fitness to do a job such as this and it's compromised, it's game over. I don't want to tarnish the angle of your book in this mood especially this week as I have to go through all my paperwork and discuss options with other lawyers.'

Later, he wrote: 'I don't know why your [sic] doing this book. In that what is in this for me? Is it to make you money for your self? I'm presuming you have a financial agenda in your motivation. Do you sell your work, I'm presuming it's in the mix for your incentive somewhere along the line. Yet for me it has not been mentioned. It's unfair to help you earn a living for free. And I get nothing yet the information and viewpoints in your book are mine, it seems a bit pointless for me moving forwards, cheers.'

Others, though, were generous with their time.

I would like to thank, then, all those who trusted me with their stories: to Boglárka, Amirah, Yuliya, Marissa, Jennifer, Zofia, Rosi, Mario, Maxine and Jasmine, Brandy, Felipe, Natalie, Arabella, Michele, and Monika.

For background and context, I'd like to extend my gratitude to Jenny Webb, Stephen Munton, Kate Clanchy, Vincent Vermeulen, Laura Smith, Ethan Mechare, Antoinette Daniel and Kasia Florek. Thanks also to Alice Marwick, for the cover.

If our house cleaners really are a mostly silent army, I feel privileged that they allowed me to give them voice on the page. I hope I have done them justice.

Dena didn't last, of course. Cleaning was never going to contain her for very long. I often wonder what became of her. We've had several cleaners since, a succession of kind and gentle women with strong arms, who never stayed in the job very long, I hope not because the weekly mess we managed to make proved insurmountable for them.

In the last few months, we've decided to no longer employ one, in part as a result of conversations with some of those I spoke to for this book. We thought it important to teach our teenage children how to clean up after themselves, before it was too late.

And so that's what we are currently attempting to do: four people struggling with a task that one woman did alone, and uncomplainingly, week after week after week.

So far, it's not going well.

Index

Nick Duerden is a writer and journalist whose work has appeared in *The Guardian*, the *Sunday Times*, the *Daily Telegraph*, the *i* paper, *GQ*, *Esquire* and *Elle*.

His previous books include *Get Well Soon: Adventures in Alternative Healthcare*, *A Life Less Lonely*, and *The Smallest Things: On the Enduring Power of Family*. He lives in London with his wife and two daughters.